D1111359

THE SERVANT OF TWO MASTERS

A Comedy

By

CARLO GOLDONI

Timeless📖Classics

THE SERVANT OF TWO MASTERS

A Comedy
By Carlo Goldoni

Translated
By Edward J. Dent

Timeless📖Classics
Editor: B. K. De Fabris

Copyright © 2014 B. K. De Fabris

CHARACTERS

PANTALONE DEI BISOGNOSI, a Venetian merchant

CLARICE, his daughter

DOCTOR LOMBARDI

SILVIO, his son

BEATRICE RASPONI, a lady of Turin, disguised as her brother
Federigo Rasponi.

FLORINDO ARETUSI, of Turin, lover of Beatrice

BRIGHELLA, an Innkeeper

SMERALDINA, maidservant to Clarice

TRUFFALDINO, servant first to Beatrice, and afterwards to
Florindo

FIRST WAITER

SECOND WAITER

FIRST PORTER

SECOND PORTER

The scene is laid in Venice.

SCENES

ACT I

Scene I:	A Room in the House of Pantalone.
Scene II:	A Street with Brighella's Inn.
Scene III:	A Room in the House of Pantalone.

ACT II

Scene I:	The Courtyard of Pantalone's House.
Scene II:	A Room in Brighella's Inn.
Scene III:	A Street with Brighella's Inn.

ACT III

Scene I:	A Room in Brighella's Inn.
Scene II:	A Street.
Scene III:	A Room in Brighella's Inn.
Scene IV:	A Room in the House of Pantalone.

ACT I

SCENE I
A room in the house of Pantalone.

Pantalone, Lombardi, Clarice, Silvio, Brighella, Smeraldina.

SILVIO. *(Offering his hand to CLARICE.)* Here is my hand, and with it I give you my whole heart.

PANTALONE. *(To CLARICE.)* Come, come, not so shy, give him your hand too. Then you will be betrothed, and very soon you shall be married.

CLARICE. Dear Silvio, here is my hand. I promise to be your wife.

SILVIO. And I promise to be your husband. *(They take hands.)*

LOMBARDI. Well said. Now that is settled, and there's no going back on it.

SMERALDINA. *(Aside.)* There's luck for you! And me just bursting to get married!

PANTALONE. *(To BRIGHELLA and SMERALDINA.)* You two shall be witnesses of this betrothal of my daughter Clarice to Signor Silvio, the worthy son of our good Doctor Lombardi!

BRIGHELLA. *(To PANTALONE.)* We will, sir, and I thank you for the honour.

PANTALONE. Look you, I was a witness at your wedding, and now you are a witness to my daughter's. I have asked no great company of friends and relations, for the Doctor too is a man of my sort. We will have dinner together; we will enjoy ourselves and nobody shall disturb us. *(To CLARICE and SILVIO.)* What say you, children, does that suit you?

SILVIO. I desire nothing better than to be near my beloved bride.

SMERALDINA. *(Aside.)* Yes, that's the best of all foods.

LOMBARDI. My son is no lover of vanities. He is an honest lad; he loves your daughter and thinks of nothing else.

PANTALONE. Truly we may say that this marriage was made in Heaven, for had it not been for the death of Federigo Rasponi, my correspondent at Turin, you know, I had promised my daughter to him, and *(To SILVIO.)* I could not then have given her to my dear son-in-law.

SILVIO. I can call myself fortunate indeed, sir; I know not if Signora Clarice will say the same.

CLARICE. You wrong me, dear Silvio. You should know if I love you. I should have married Signor Rasponi in obedience to my father; but my heart has always been yours.

LOMBARDI. 'Tis true indeed, the will of Heaven is wrought in unexpected ways. *(To PANTALONE.)* Pray, sir, how did Federigo Rasponi come to die?

PANTALONE. Poor wretch, I hardly know. He was killed one night on account of some affair about his sister. Someone ran a sword through him and that was the end of him.

BRIGHELLA. Did that happen at Turin, sir?

PANTALONE. At Turin.

BRIGHELLA. Alas, poor gentleman! I am indeed sorry to hear it.

PANTALONE. *(To BRIGHELLA.)* Did you know Signor Federigo Rasponi?

BRIGHELLA. Indeed and I did, sir. I was three years at Turin. I knew his sister too—a fine high-spirited young woman— dressed like a man and rode a-horseback; and he loved her more than anyone in the world. Lord! who'ld ha' thought it?

PANTALONE. Well, misfortune waits for all of us. But come, let us talk no more of sad things. Do you know what I have in mind, good master Brighella? I know you love to show your skill in the kitchen. Now, I would have you make us a few dishes of your best.

BRIGHELLA. 'Tis a pleasure to serve you, sir. Though I say it that shouldn't, customers are always well contented at my house. They say there's no place where they eat as they do there. You shall taste something fine, sir.

PANTALONE. Good, good. Let's have something with plenty of gravy that we can sop the bread in. *(A knock at the door.)* Oh! someone is knocking. Smeraldina, see who it is.

SMERALDINA. Yes, sir. *(She goes to the door.)*

CLARICE. *(Wishing to retire.)* Sir, may I beg your leave?

PANTALONE. Wait; we are all coming. Let us hear who is there.

SMERALDINA. *(Coming back.)* Sir, there is a gentleman's servant below who desires to give you a message. He would tell me nothing. He says he would speak to the master.

PANTALONE. Tell him to come up. We'll hear what he has to say.

SMERALDINA. I'll fetch him, sir. *(Exits.)*

CLARICE. May I not go, sir?

PANTALONE. Whither then, madam?

CLARICE. I know not—to my own room—

PANTALONE. No, madam, no; you stay here. *(Aside to LOMBARDI.)* These love-birds can't be left alone just yet for a while.

LOMBARDI. *(Aside to PANTALONE.)* Prudence above all things!

SMERALDINA brings in TRUFFALDINO.

TRUFFALDINO. My most humble duty to the ladies and gentlemen. And a very fine company too, to be sure! Very fine, indeed!

PANTALONE. Who are you, my good friend? And what is your business?

TRUFFALDINO. *(To PANTALONE, pointing to CLARICE.)* Who is this fair gentlewoman?

PANTALONE. That is my daughter.

TRUFFALDINO. Delighted to hear it.

SMERALDINA. *(To TRUFFALDINO.)* What's more, she is going to be married.

TRUFFALDINO. I'm sorry to hear it. And who are you?

SMERALDINA. I am her maid, sir.

TRUFFALDINO. I congratulate her.

PANTALONE. Come, sir, have done with ceremony. What do you want with me? Who are you? Who sends you hither?

TRUFFALDINO. Patience, patience, my good sir, take it easy. Three questions at once is too much for a poor man.

PANTALONE. *(Aside to LOMBARDI.)* I think the man's a fool.

LOMBARDI. *(Aside to PANTALONE.)* I think he's playing the fool.

TRUFFALDINO. *(To SMERALDINA.)* Is it you that are going to be married?

SMERALDINA. *(Sighs.)* No, sir.

PANTALONE. Will you tell me who you are, or will you go about your business?

TRUFFALDINO. If you only want to know who I am, I'll tell you in two words. I am the servant of my master. *(Turns to SMERALDINA.)* To go back to what I was saying—

PANTALONE. But who is your master?

TRUFFALDINO. *(To PANTALONE.)* He is a gentleman who desires the honour of paying his respects to you. *(To SMERALDINA.)* We must have a talk about this marriage.

PANTALONE. Who is this gentleman, I say? What is his name?

TRUFFALDINO. Oh, that's a long story. Si'or Federigo Rasponi of Turin, that's my master, and he sends his compliments, and he has come to see you, and he's down below, and he sends me to say that he would like to come up and he's waiting for an answer. Anything else, or will that do? *(All look surprised. TRUFFALDINO turns to SMERALDINA, as before.)* Let's begin again.

PANTALONE. Come here and talk to me. What the devil do you mean?

TRUFFALDINO. And if you want to know who I am, I am Truffaldin' Battocchio from Bergamo.

PANTALONE. I don't care who you are. Tell me again, who is this master of yours? I fear I did not hear you rightly.

TRUFFALDINO. Poor old gentleman! he must be deaf. My master is Si'or Federigo Rasponi of Turin.

PANTALONE. Away! You must be mad. Signor Federigo Rasponi of Turin is dead.

TRUFFALDINO. Dead?

PANTALONE. To be sure he's dead, worse luck for him.

TRUFFALDINO. *(Aside.)* The devil! my Master dead? why, I left him alive downstairs! *(To PANTALONE.)* You really mean he is dead?

PANTALONE. I tell you for an absolute certainty, he is dead.

LOMBARDI. 'Tis the honest truth; he is dead; we can have no doubt about it.

TRUFFALDINO. *(Aside.)* Alas my poor master! He must have met with an accident. *(To PANTALONE, as if retiring.)* Your very humble servant, sir.

PANTALONE. Can I do nothing more for you?

TRUFFALDINO. If he's dead, there's nothing more to do. *(Aside.)* But I'm going to see if it's true or not. *(Exits.)*

PANTALONE. What are we to make of this fellow? Is he knave

or fool?

LOMBARDI. I really don't know. Probably a little of both.

BRIGHELLA. I should say he was just a zany. He comes from Bergamo; I can't think he is a knave.

SMERALDINA. He's not such a fool, neither. *(Aside.)* I like that little dark fellow.

PANTALONE. But what is this nightmare about Signor Federigo?

CLARICE. If 'tis true indeed that he is here, it would be the worst of news for me.

PANTALONE. What nonsense! did not you see the letters yourself?

SILVIO. If he is alive and here after all, he has come too late.

Re-enter TRUFFALDINO.

TRUFFALDINO. Gentlemen, I am surprised at you. Is that the way to treat a poor man? Is that the way you deceive strangers? Is that the behaviour of a gentleman? I shall insist upon satisfaction.

PANTALONE. *(To LOMBARDI.)* We must be careful, the man's mad. *(To TRUFFALDINO.)* What's the matter? What have they done to you?

TRUFFALDINO. To go and tell me that Si'or Federigo Rasponi was dead!

PANTALONE. Well, what then?

TRUFFALDINO. What then? Well, he's here, safe and sound, in good health and spirits, and he desires to pay his respects to you with your kind permission.

PANTALONE. Signor Federigo?

TRUFFALDINO. Si'or Federigo.

PANTALONE. Rasponi?

TRUFFALDINO. Rasponi.

PANTALONE. Of Turin?

TRUFFALDINO. Of Turin.

PANTALONE. Be off to Bedlam, my lad; that's the place for you.

TRUFFALDINO. The Devil take you there, sir! you'll make me swear like a Turk. I tell you he's here, in the house, in the next room, bad luck to you.

PANTALONE. If you say any more I'll break your head.

LOMBARDI. No, no, Signor Pantalone; I tell you what to do. Tell him to bring in this person whom he thinks to be Federigo Rasponi.

PANTALONE. Well, bring in this man that is risen from the dead.

TRUFFALDINO. He may have been dead and risen from the dead, for all I know. That's no affair of mine. But he's alive now, sure enough, and you shall see him with your own eyes. I'll go and tell him to come. *(Angrily to PANTALONE.)* And 'tis time you learned how to behave properly to strangers, to gentlemen of my position, to honourable citizens of Bergamo. *(To SMERALDINA.)* Young woman, we will have some talk together when you will. *(Exits.)*

CLARICE. Silvio, I am all of a tremble.

SILVIO. Have no fear; whatever happens you shall be mine.

LOMBARDI. Now we shall discover the truth.

PANTALONE. Some rogue, I dare say, come to tell me a string of lies.

BRIGHELLA. Sir, as I told you just now, I knew Signor Federigo; we shall see if it be he.

SMERALDINA. *(Aside.)* That little dark fellow doesn't look like a liar. I wonder, now, if—*(Curtsey to PANTALONE.)* By you good leave, sir. *(Exits.)*

BEATRICE enters, dressed as a man.

BEATRICE. Signor Pantalone, that courtesy which I have so much admired in your correspondence is but ill matched in the treatment which I have received from you in person. I send my servant to pay you my respects, and you keep me standing in the street for half an hour before you condescend to allow me to enter.

PANTALONE. *(Nervously.)* I ask your pardon. But, sir, who are you?

BEATRICE. Your obedient servant, sir, Federigo Rasponi of Turin. *(All look bewildered.)*

PANTALONE. Extraordinary!

BRIGHELLA. *(Aside.)* What does this mean? This is not

Federigo, this is his sister Beatrice.

PANTALONE. I rejoice to see you, sir, alive and in health, after the bad news which we had received. *(Aside to LOMBARDI.)* I tell you, I am not convinced yet.

BEATRICE. I know; 'twas reported that I was killed in a duel. Heaven be praised, I was but wounded; and no sooner was I restored to health, than I set out for Venice, according to our previous arrangement.

PANTALONE. I don't know what to say. You have the appearance of an honest man, sir; but I have sure and certain evidence that Signor Federigo is dead, and you will understand—that if you cannot give us proof of the contrary—

BEATRICE. Your doubt is most natural; I recognise that I must give you proof of my identity. Here are four letters from correspondents of yours whom you know personally; one of them is from the manager of our Bank. You will recognise the signatures and you will satisfy yourself as to who I am. *(She gives four letters to PANTALONE who reads them to himself.)*

CLARICE. Ah, Silvio, we are lost.

SILVIO. I will lose my life before I lose you.

BEATRICE. *(Noticing BRIGHELLA, aside.)* Heavens! Brighella! How the devil does he come to be here? If he betrays me—*(Aloud to BRIGHELLA.)* Friend, I think I know you.

BRIGHELLA. Indeed yes, sir; do you not remember Brighella Cavicchio at Turin?

BEATRICE. Ah yes, now I recognise you. *(Goes up to him.)* And what are you doing in Venice, my good fellow? *(Aside to BRIGHELLA.)* For the love of heaven do not betray me.

BRIGHELLA. *(Aside to BEATRICE.)* Trust me. *(Aloud.)* I keep an inn, sir, at your service.

BEATRICE. The very thing for me; as I have the pleasure of your acquaintance, I shall come to lodge at your inn.

BRIGHELLA. You do me honour, sir. *(Aside.)* Running contraband, I'll be bound.

PANTALONE. I have read the letters. Certainly they present Signor Federigo Rasponi to me, and if you present them, I am bound to believe that you are—the person named therein.

BEATRICE. If you are still in doubt, here is master Brighella; he knows me, he can assure you as to who I am.

BRIGHELLA. Of course, sir, I am happy to assure you.

PANTALONE. Well, if that be so, and my good friend Brighella confirms the testimony of the letters, then, dear Signor Federigo, I am delighted to see you and I ask your pardon for having doubted your word.

CLARICE. Then, sir, this gentleman is indeed Signor Federigo Rasponi?

PANTALONE. But of course he is.

CLARICE. *(Aside to SILVIO.)* Oh misery, what will happen to us?

SILVIO. *(Aside to CLARICE.)* Don't be frightened; you are mine and I will protect you.

PANTALONE. *(Aside to LOMBARDI.)* What do you say to it, Doctor? He has come just in the nick of time.

LOMBARDI. Accidit in puncto, quod non contingit in anno.

BEATRICE. *(Pointing to CLARICE.)* Signor Pantalone, who is that young lady?

PANTALONE. That is my daughter Clarice.

BEATRICE. The one who was promised in marriage to me?

PANTALONE. Precisely, sir; that is she. *(Aside.)* Now I am in a pretty mess.

BEATRICE. *(To CLARICE.)* Madam, permit me to have the honour.

CLARICE. *(Stiffly.)* Your most humble servant, sir.

BEATRICE. *(To PANTALONE.)* She receives me somewhat coldly.

PANTALONE. You must forgive her, she is shy by nature.

BEATRICE. *(To PANTALONE, pointing at SILVIO.)* And this gentleman is a relative of yours?

PANTALONE. Yes, sir; he is a nephew of mine.

SILVIO. *(To BEATRICE.)* No, sir, I am not his nephew at all; I am the promised husband of Signora Clarice.

LOMBARDI. *(Aside to SILVIO.)* Well said, my boy! Don't lose your chance! Stand up for your rights, but do nothing rash.

BEATRICE. What? You the promised husband of Signora Clarice? Was she not promised to me?

PANTALONE. There, there, I'll explain the whole matter. My

8

dear Signor Federigo, I fully believed that the story of your accident was true, that you were dead, in fact, and so I had promised my daughter to Signor Silvio; but there is not the least harm done. You have arrived at last, just in time. Clarice is yours, if you will have her, and I am here to keep my word. Signor Silvio, I don't know what to say; you can see the position yourself. You remember what I said to you; and you will have no cause to bear me ill-will.

SILVIO. But Signor Federigo will never consent to take a bride who has given her hand to another.

BEATRICE. Oh, I am not so fastidious. I will take her in spite of that. *(Aside.)* I mean to have some fun out of this.

LOMBARDI. There's a fine fashionable husband! I like him.

BEATRICE. I hope Signora Clarice will not refuse me her hand.

SILVIO. Come, sir, you have arrived too late. Signora Clarice is to be my wife, and you need have no hope that I will yield her to you. If Signor Pantalone does me wrong, I will be avenged upon him; and whoever presumes to desire Clarice will have to fight for her against this sword.

LOMBARDI. *(Aside.)* That's a fine boy, by the Lord!

BEATRICE. *(Aside.)* Thank you, but I don't mean to die just yet.

LOMBARDI. Sir, I must beg to inform you that you are too late. Signora Clarice is to marry my son. The law, the law, sir, is clear on the point. Prior in tempore, potior in jure.

(LOMBARDI and SILVIO exit.)

BEATRICE. *(To CLARICE.)* And you, madam bride, do you say nothing?

CLARICE. I say—I say—I'd sooner marry the hangman. *(Exits.)*

PANTALONE. What, you minx! what did you say? *(Starts to run after her.)*

BEATRICE. Stay, Signor Pantalone; I am sorry for her. It is not the moment for severity. In course of time I hope I may deserve her favour. Meanwhile let us go into our accounts together, for, as you know, that is one of the two reasons that have brought me to Venice.

PANTALONE. Everything is in order for our inspection. You shall see the books; your money is ready for you, and we will make up the account whenever you like.

BEATRICE. I will call on you at some more convenient time.

Now, if you will allow me, I will go with Brighella to settle some little business which I have to do.

PANTALONE. You shall do as you please, and if you have need of anything, I am at your service.

BEATRICE. Well, if you could give me a little money, I should be greatly obliged. I did not bring any with me, for fear of being robbed on the way.

PANTALONE. I am delighted to serve you; but the cashier is not here just now. The moment he comes I will send the money to your lodgings. Are you not staying at my friend Brighella's?

BEATRICE. Yes, I lie there. But I will send my servant; he is entirely honest. You can trust him with anything.

PANTALONE. Very well. I will carry out your wishes, and if you may be pleased to take pot luck with me, I am yours to command.

BEATRICE. For to-day I thank you. Another day I shall be happy to wait upon you.

PANTALONE. Then I shall expect you.

Enter SMERALDINA.

SMERALDINA. *(To PANTALONE.)* Sir, you are asked for.

PANTALONE. Who is it?

SMERALDINA. I couldn't say, Sir.

PANTALONE. I will come directly. Sir, I beg you to excuse me. Brighella, you are at home here; be good enough to attend Signor Federigo.

BEATRICE. Pray do not put yourself about for me, sir.

PANTALONE. I must go. Farewell, sir. *(Aside.)* I don't want to have trouble in my house. *(Exits with SMERALDINA.)*

BRIGHELLA. May I ask, Signora Beatrice—?

BEATRICE. Hush, for the love of Heaven, don't betray me. My poor brother is dead. 'Twas thought Florindo Aretusi killed him in a duel. You remember, Florindo loved me, and my brother would not have it. They fought, Federigo fell, and Florindo fled from justice. I heard he was making for Venice, so I put on my brother's clothes and followed him. Thanks to the letters of credit, which are my brother's, and thanks still more to you, Signor Pantalone takes me for

Federigo. We are to make up our accounts; I shall draw the money, and then I shall be able to help Florindo too, if he has need of it. Be my friend, dear Brighella, help me, please! You shall be generously rewarded.

BRIGHELLA. That's all very well, but I don't want to be responsible for Signor Pantalone paying you out money in good faith and then finding himself made a fool of.

BEATRICE. Made a fool of? If my brother is dead, am I not his heir?

BRIGHELLA. Very true. Then why not say so?

BEATRICE. If I do that, I can do nothing. Pantalone will begin by treating me as if he were my guardian; then they will all worry me and say my conduct is unbecoming and all that sort of thing. I want my liberty. Help me to it. 'Twill not last long.

BRIGHELLA. Well, well, you were always one for having your own way. Trust me, and I'll do my best for you.

BEATRICE. Thank you. And now let us go to your inn.

BRIGHELLA. Where is your servant?

BEATRICE. I told him to wait for me in the street.

BRIGHELLA. Wherever did you get hold of that idiot? He cannot even speak plain.

BEATRICE. I picked him up on the journey. He seems a fool at times; but he isn't really a fool and I can rely on his loyalty.

BRIGHELLA. Yes, loyalty's a fine thing. Well, I am at your service. To think what love will make people do!

BEATRICE. Oh, this is nothing. Love makes people do far worse things than this.

BRIGHELLA. Well, here's a good beginning. If you go on that way, Lord knows what may come of it.

BEATRICE and BRIGHELLA exit.

SCENE II
A street with Brighella's Inn.

TRUFFALDINO solus.

TRUFFALDINO. I'm sick of waiting; I can hold out no longer.

With this master of mine there's not enough to eat, and the less there is the more I want it. The town clock struck twelve half an hour ago, and my belly struck two hours ago at least. If I only knew where we were going to lodge! With my other masters the first thing they did, as soon as they came to a town, was to go to a tavern. This gentleman— Lord no! he leaves his trunks in the boat at the landing-stage, goes off to pay visits and forgets all about his poor servant. When they say we ought to serve our masters with love, they ought to tell the masters to have a little charity towards their servants. Here's an inn. I've half a mind to go in and see if I could find something to tickle my teeth; but what if my master comes to look for me? His own fault; he ought to know better. I'll go in—but now I come to think of it, there's another little difficulty that I hadn't remembered; I haven't a penny. Oh poor Truffaldin'! Rather than be a servant, devil take me, I'd—what indeed? By the grace of Heaven there's nothing I can do.

Enter FLORINDO in travelling dress with a PORTER carrying a trunk on his shoulder.

PORTER. I tell you, sir, I can go no farther; the weight's enough to kill me.

FLORINDO. Here is the sign of an inn. Can't you carry it these few steps?

PORTER. Help! the trunk is falling.

FLORINDO. I told you you could not carry it; you're too weak; you have no strength at all. *(FLORINDO re-arranges the trunk on the Porter's shoulder.)*

TRUFFALDINO. Here's a chance for sixpence. *(To FLORINDO.)* Sir, can I do anything for you?

FLORINDO. My good man, be so good as to carry this trunk into the inn there.

TRUFFALDINO. Yes, sir, let me take it, sir. See how I do it. *(To the PORTER.)* You be off! *(TRUFFALDINO puts his shoulder under the trunk and takes it by himself, knocking the PORTER. down at the same time.)*

FLORINDO. Well done!

TRUFFALDINO. It weighs nothing. A mere trifle. *(He goes into the inn with the trunk.)*

FLORINDO. *(To PORTER.)* There! You see how it's done.

PORTER. I can do no more. I work as a porter for my misfortune, but I am the son of a respectable person.

FLORINDO. What did your father do?

PORTER. My father? He skinned lambs in the town.

FLORINDO. The fellow's mad. *(To PORTER.)* That will do. *(Goes towards the inn.)*

PORTER. Please your honour—

FLORINDO. What do you want?

PORTER. The money for the porterage.

FLORINDO. How much am I to give you for ten yards? There's the landing-stage! *(Pointing off.)*

PORTER. I didn't count them. I want my pay. *(Holds out his hand.)*

FLORINDO. There's twopence. *(Gives money.)*

PORTER. I want my pay. *(Still holding out his hand.)*

FLORINDO. Lord, what obstinacy! Here's twopence more. *(Gives money.)*

PORTER. I want my pay.

FLORINDO. *(Kicks him.)* Go and be hanged!

PORTER. Thank you, sir, that's enough. *(Exits.)*

FLORINDO. There's a humorous fellow! He was positively waiting for me to kick him. Well, let us go and see what the inn is like—

Re-enter TRUFFALDINO.

TRUFFALDINO. Sir, everything is ready for you.

FLORINDO. What lodging is there here?

TRUFFALDINO. 'Tis a very good place, sir. Good beds, fine looking-glasses, and a grand kitchen with a smell to it that is very comforting. I have talked with the waiter. You will be served like a king.

FLORINDO. What's your trade?

TRUFFALDINO. Servant.

FLORINDO. Are you a Venetian?

TRUFFALDINO. Not from Venice, but of the State. I'm from Bergamo, at your service.

FLORINDO. Have you a master now?

TRUFFALDINO. At the moment—to tell the truth, I have not.

FLORINDO. You are without a master?

TRUFFALDINO. You see me, sir. I am without a master. *(Aside.)* My master is not here, so I tell no lies.

FLORINDO. Will you come and be my servant?

TRUFFALDINO. Why not? *(Aside.)* If his terms are better.

FLORINDO. At any rate, for as long as I stay in Venice.

TRUFFALDINO. Very good, sir. How much will you give me?

FLORINDO. How much do you want?

TRUFFALDINO. I'll tell you: another master I had, who is here no more, he gave me a shilling a day and all found.

FLORINDO. Good, I will give you as much.

TRUFFALDINO. You must give me a little more than that.

FLORINDO. How much more do you want?

TRUFFALDINO. A halfpenny a day for snuff.

FLORINDO. Oh, I'll give you that and welcome.

TRUFFALDINO. If that's so, I'm your man, sir.

FLORINDO. But I should like to know a little more about you.

TRUFFALDINO. If you want to know all about me, you go to Bergamo; anyone there will tell you who I am.

FLORINDO. Have you nobody in Venice who knows you?

TRUFFALDINO. I only arrived this morning, sir.

FLORINDO. Well, well, I take you for an honest man. I will give you a trial.

TRUFFALDINO. You give me a trial and you shall see.

FLORINDO. First of all, I am anxious to know if there are letters at the Post for me. Here is half a crown; go to the Turin Post and ask if there are letters for Florindo Aretusi; if there are, take them and bring them at once. I shall wait for you.

TRUFFALDINO. Meanwhile you will order dinner, sir?

FLORINDO. Yes, well said! I will order it. *(Aside.)* He is a wag, I like him. I'll give him a trial.

FLORINDO goes into the inn.

TRUFFALDINO. A halfpenny more a day, that's fifteen pence a month. 'Tis not true that the other gentleman gave me a shilling; he gives me six pennies. Maybe six pennies make a shilling, but I'm not quite sure. And this gentleman from Turin is nowhere to be seen. He's mad. He's a young fellow without a beard and without any sense neither. He may go about his business; I shall go to the Post for my new gentleman.

As he is going, BEATRICE enters with BRIGHELLA and meets him.

BEATRICE. That's a nice way to behave! Is that the way you wait for me?

TRUFFALDINO. Here I am, sir. I am still waiting for you.

BEATRICE. And how do you come to be waiting for me here, and not in the street where I told you? 'Tis a mere accident that I have found you.

TRUFFALDINO. I went for a bit of a walk to take away my appetite.

BEATRICE. Well, go at once to the landing-stage; fetch my trunk and take it to the inn of Master Brighella.

BRIGHELLA. There's my inn, you cannot mistake it.

BEATRICE. Very well then, make haste, and I will wait for you.

TRUFFALDINO. The devil! In that inn?

BEATRICE. Here, you will go at the same time to the Turin Post and ask if there are any letters for me. You may ask if there are letters for Federigo Rasponi and also for Beatrice Rasponi. That's my sister. Some friend of hers might perhaps write to her; so be sure to see if there are letters either for her or for me.

TRUFFALDINO. *(Aside.)* What am I to do? Here's a pretty kettle of fish!

BRIGHELLA. *(To BEATRICE.)* Why do you expect letters in your real name if you left home secretly?

BEATRICE. I told the steward to write to me; and I don't know which name he may use. I'll tell you more later. *(To TRUFFALDINO.)* Make haste, be off with you to the Post and the landing-stage. Fetch the letters and have the trunk brought to the inn; I shall be there. *(BEATRICE exits into the inn.)*

TRUFFALDINO. Are you the landlord?

BRIGHELLA. Yes, I am. You behave properly and you need have no fear, I will do you well. *(BRIGHELLA exits into the inn.)*

TRUFFALDINO. There's luck! There are many that look in vain for a master, and I have found two. What the devil am I to do? I cannot wait upon them both. No? Why not? Wouldn't it be a fine thing to wait upon both of them, earn two men's wages and eat and drink for two? 'Twould be a fine thing indeed, if neither of them found it out. And if they did? what then? No matter! If one sends me away, I stay with the other. I swear I'll try it. If it last but a day, I'll try it. Whatever happens I shall have done a fine thing. Here goes. Let's go to the Post for both of 'em.

Enter SILVIO and meets TRUFFALDINO.

SILVIO. *(Aside.)* That is the servant of Federigo Rasponi. *(To TRUFFALDINO.)* My good man.

TRUFFALDINO. Sir?

SILVIO. Where is your master?

TRUFFALDINO. My master? He's in that inn there.

SILVIO. Go at once and tell your master that I wish to speak to him; if he be a man of honour let him come down; I wait for him.

TRUFFALDINO. My dear sir—

SILVIO. *(Angrily.)* Go at once.

TRUFFALDINO. But I must tell you, my master—

SILVIO. Don't answer me; or, by Heaven, I'll—

TRUFFALDINO. But which do you want?

SILVIO. At once, I say, or I'll beat you.

TRUFFALDINO. *(Aside.)* Well, I don't know—I'll send the first I can find. *(TRUFFALDINO exits into the inn.)*

SILVIO. No, I will never suffer the presence of a rival. Federigo may have got off once with his life, but he shall not always have the same fortune. Either he shall renounce all claims to Clarice, or he shall give me the satisfaction of a gentleman. Here are some more people coming out of the inn. I don't want to be disturbed. *(Retires to the opposite side.)*

Enter TRUFFALDINO with FLORINDO.

16

TRUFFALDINO. *(Points out SILVIO to FLORINDO.)* There's the fire-eating gentleman, sir.

FLORINDO. I do not know him. What does he want with me?

TRUFFALDINO. I don't know. I go to fetch the letters, with your good leave, sir. *(Aside.)* I don't want any more trouble. *(Exits.)*

SILVIO. *(Aside.)* Federigo does not come?

FLORINDO. *(Aside.)* I must find out what the truth is. *(To SILVIO.)* Sir, are you the gentleman who inquired for me?

SILVIO. I, sir? I have not even the honour of your acquaintance.

FLORINDO. But that servant who has just gone told me that with a loud and threatening voice you made bold to challenge me.

SILVIO. He misunderstood. I said I wished to speak to his master.

FLORINDO. Very well, I am his master.

SILVIO. You his master?

FLORINDO. Certainly. He is in my service.

SILVIO. Then I ask your pardon. Either your servant is exactly like another whom I saw this morning, or he waits on another person.

FLORINDO. You may set your mind at rest; he waits on me.

SILVIO. If that be so, I ask your pardon again.

FLORINDO. No harm done. Mistakes often occur.

SILVIO. Are you a stranger here, sir?

FLORINDO. From Turin, sir, at your service.

SILVIO. The man whom I would have provoked was from Turin.

FLORINDO. Then perhaps I may know him; if he has given you offence, I shall gladly assist you to obtain just satisfaction.

SILVIO. Do you know one Federigo Rasponi?

FLORINDO. Ah! I knew him only too well.

SILVIO. He makes claim, on the strength of her father's word, to the lady who this morning swore to be my wife.

FLORINDO. My good friend, Federigo Rasponi cannot take your wife away from you. He is dead.

SILVIO. Yes, we all believed that he was dead; but this morning to my disgust he arrived in Venice safe and sound.

FLORINDO. Sir, you petrify me.

SILVIO. No wonder! I was petrified myself.

FLORINDO. I assure you Federigo Rasponi is dead.

SILVIO. I assure you that Federigo Rasponi is alive.

FLORINDO. Take care you are not deceived.

SILVIO. Signor Pantalone dei Bisognosi, the young lady's father, has made all possible inquiries to assure himself and is in possession of incontestable proofs that he is here in person.

FLORINDO. *(Aside.)* Then he was not killed in the duel, as everybody believed!

SILVIO. Either he or I must renounce claim to the love of Clarice or to life.

FLORINDO. *(Aside.)* Federigo here?

SILVIO. I am surprised that you have not seen him. He was to lodge at this very inn.

FLORINDO. I have not seen him. They told me that there was no one else at all staying there.

SILVIO. He must have changed his mind. Forgive me, sir, if I have troubled you. If you see him, tell him, that for his own welfare he must abandon the idea of this marriage. Silvio Lombardi is my name. I am your most obedient servant, sir.

FLORINDO. I shall be greatly pleased to have the honour of your friendship. *(Aside.)* I am confounded.

SILVIO. May I beg to know your name, sir?

FLORINDO. *(Aside.)* I must not discover myself. *(To SILVIO.)* Your servant, sir, Orazio Ardenti.

SILVIO. Signor Orazio, I am yours to command. *(Exits.)*

FLORINDO. I was told he died on the spot. Yet I fled so hurriedly when accused of the crime that I had no chance of finding out the truth. Then, since he is not dead, it will be better for me to go back to Turin and console my beloved Beatrice, who is perhaps in suffering and sorrow for my absence.

Enter TRUFFALDINO with another PORTER who carries Beatrice's trunk. TRUFFALDINO comes forward a few steps, sees FLORINDO, and fearing to be seen himself, makes the PORTER retire.

TRUFFALDINO. Come along. This way—The devil! There's my other master. Go back, friend, and wait for me at that corner.

The PORTER exits.

FLORINDO. *(Continuing to himself.)* Yes, without delay. I will go back to Turin.

TRUFFALDINO. Here I am, sir.

FLORINDO. Truffaldino, will you come to Turin with me?

TRUFFALDINO. When?

FLORINDO. Now; at once.

TRUFFALDINO. Before dinner?

FLORINDO. No, we will have dinner, and then we will go.

TRUFFALDINO. Very good, sir. I'll think it over at dinner.

FLORINDO. Have you been to the Post?

TRUFFALDINO. Yes, sir.

FLORINDO. Have you found my letters?

TRUFFALDINO. I have, sir.

FLORINDO. Where are they?

TRUFFALDINO. I will give you them. *(Takes three letters out of his pocket. Aside.)* The devil! I have mixed up one master's letters with the other's. How shall I find out which are his? I cannot read.

FLORINDO. Come, give me my letters.

TRUFFALDINO. Directly, sir. *(Aside.)* Here's a muddle. *(To FLORINDO.)* I must tell you, sir; these three letters are not all for your honour. I met another servant, who knows me; we were in service together at Bergamo; I told him I was going to the Post, and he asked me to see whether there was anything for his master. I think there was one letter, but I don't know which of them it was.

FLORINDO. Let me see; I will take mine and give you the other back.

TRUFFALDINO. There, sir; I only wanted to do my friend a good turn.

FLORINDO. *(Aside.)* What is this? A letter addressed to Beatrice Rasponi? To Beatrice Rasponi at Venice?

TRUFFALDINO. Did you find the one that belongs to my mate?

FLORINDO. Who is this mate of yours who asked you to do this for him?

TRUFFALDINO. He is a servant—his name is Pasqual'—

FLORINDO. Whom does he wait upon?

TRUFFALDINO. I do not know, sir.

FLORINDO. But if he told you to fetch his master's letters, he must have told you his name.

TRUFFALDINO. Of course he did. *(Aside.)* The muddle's getting thicker.

FLORINDO. Well, what name did he tell you?

TRUFFALDINO. I don't remember.

FLORINDO. What?

TRUFFALDINO. He wrote it down on a bit of paper.

FLORINDO. And where is the paper?

TRUFFALDINO. I left it at the Post.

FLORINDO. *(Aside.)* Confusion! What does this mean?

TRUFFALDINO. *(Aside.)* I am learning my part as I go along.

FLORINDO. Where does this fellow Pasquale live?

TRUFFALDINO. Indeed, sir, I haven't the slightest idea.

FLORINDO. How will you be able to give him the letter?

TRUFFALDINO. He said he would meet me in the Piazza.

FLORINDO. *(Aside.)* I don't know what to make of it.

TRUFFALDINO. *(Aside.)* If I get through this business clean 'twill be a miracle. *(To FLORINDO.)* Pray give me the letter, sir, and I shall find him somewhere.

FLORINDO. No; I mean to open this letter.

TRUFFALDINO. Oh, sir, do not do that, sir. Besides, you know how wrong it is to open letters.

FLORINDO. I care not. This letter interests me too much. It is addressed to a person on whom I have a certain claim. I can open it without scruple. *(He opens the letter.)*

TRUFFALDINO. As you will, sir. *(Aside.)* He has opened it!

FLORINDO. *(Reads.)* Madam, your departure from this city has given rise to much talk, and all understand that you have gone to join Signor Florindo. The Court of Justice has discovered that you have fled in man's dress and intends to have you arrested. I have not sent this letter by the courier from Turin to Venice, so as not to reveal the place whither you were bound, but I have sent it to a friend at Genoa to be forwarded to Venice. If I have any more news to tell you, I will not fail to send it by the same means. Your most humble servant, Antonio.

TRUFFALDINO. That's a nice way to behave! Reading other people's letters!

FLORINDO. *(Aside.)* What is all this? Beatrice has left home? in man's dress? to join me? Indeed she loves me. Heaven grant I may find her in Venice. *(To TRUFFALDINO.)* Here, my good Truffaldino, go and do all you can to find Pasquale. Find out from him who his master is, and if he be man or woman. Find out where he lodges, and if you can, bring him here to me, and both he and you shall be handsomely rewarded.

TRUFFALDINO. Give me the letter; I will try to find him.

FLORINDO. There it is. I count upon you. This matter is of infinite importance to me.

TRUFFALDINO. But am I to give him the letter open like this?

FLORINDO. Tell him it was a mistake, an accident. Don't make difficulties.

TRUFFALDINO. And are you going to Turin now?

FLORINDO. No, not for the present. Lose no time. Go and find Pasquale. *(Aside.)* Beatrice in Venice, Federigo in Venice! If her brother finds her, unhappy woman! I will do all I can to discover her first. *(He exits towards the town.)*

TRUFFALDINO. Upon my word, I hope he is not going away. I want to see how my two jobs will work out. I'm on my mettle. This letter, now, which I have to take to my other master—I do not like to have to give it to him opened. I must try to fold it again. (*Tries various awkward folds.*) And now it must be sealed. If I only knew how to do it! I have seen my grandmother sometimes seal letters with chewed bread. I'll try it. (*Takes a piece of bread out of his pocket.*) It's a pity to waste this little piece of bread, but still something must be done. *(Chews a little bread to seal the letter and accidentally swallows it.)* The devil! it has gone down. I must chew another bit. *(Same business.)* No good; nature rebels. I'll try once more. *(Chews again; would like to swallow the bread, but restrains himself and with great difficulty removes the bread from his mouth.)* Ah, here it is; I'll seal the letter. *(Seals the letter with the bread.)* I think that looks quite well. I'm always a great man for doing things cleanly. Lord! I had forgotten the porter. *(Calls off.)* Friend, come hither; take the trunk on your shoulder.

Re-enter the PORTER.

PORTER. Here I am. Where am I to carry it?
TRUFFALDINO. Take it into that inn. I am coming directly.

BEATRICE comes out of the inn.

BEATRICE. Is this my trunk?
TRUFFALDINO. Yes, sir.
BEATRICE. *(To the PORTER.)* Carry it into my room.
PORTER. Which is your room?
BEATRICE. Ask the waiter.
PORTER. There's one and threepence to pay.
BEATRICE. Go on, I will pay you.
PORTER. Please be quick about it.
BEATRICE. Don't bother me.
PORTER. I've half a mind to throw the trunk down in the middle
    of the street. *(Goes into the inn.)*
TRUFFALDINO. Great folk for politeness, these porters!
BEATRICE. Have you been to the Post?
TRUFFALDINO. Yes, sir.
BEATRICE. Any letters for me?
TRUFFALDINO. One for your sister.
BEATRICE. Good; where is it?
TRUFFALDINO. Here. *(Gives letter.)*
BEATRICE. This letter has been opened.
TRUFFALDINO. Opened? No! Impossible!
BEATRICE. Yes, opened, and then sealed with bread.
TRUFFALDINO. I can't think how that can have happened.
BEATRICE. You cannot think, eh? Rascal, who has opened this
    letter? I must know.
TRUFFALDINO. Sir, I'll tell you, I'll confess the truth. We are
    all liable to make mistakes. At the Post there was a letter for
    me; I can't read very much, and by mistake, instead of
    opening my letter, I opened yours. I ask your pardon—
BEATRICE. If that was all, there's no great harm done.
TRUFFALDINO. 'Tis true, on the word of a poor man.
BEATRICE. Have you read this letter? Do you know what's in
    it?

TRUFFALDINO. Not a word. I can't read the handwriting.
BEATRICE. Has anyone else seen it?
TRUFFALDINO. *(With an air of great indignation.)* Oh!
BEATRICE. Take care now—
TRUFFALDINO. *(Same business.)* Sir!
BEATRICE. *(Aside.)* I hope he is not deceiving me. *(Reads to herself.)*
TRUFFALDINO. That's all put straight.
BEATRICE. *(Aside.)* Antonio is a faithful servant and I am obliged to him. *(To TRUFFALDINO.)* Listen; I have some business to do close by. You go into the inn, open the trunk—here are my keys—and unpack my things. When I come back, we will have dinner. *(Aside.)* I have seen nothing of Signor Pantalone, and I am anxious to have my money. *(Exits.)*
TRUFFALDINO. Come, that all went well; it couldn't have gone better. I'm a great fellow. I think a deal more of myself than I did before.

Enter PANTALONE.

PANTALONE. Tell me, my good man, is your master in the house?
TRUFFALDINO. No, sir, he is not there.
PANTALONE. Do you know where he may be?
TRUFFALDINO. Not that neither.
PANTALONE. Is he coming home to dinner?
TRUFFALDINO. Yes, I should think so.
PANTALONE. Here, as soon as he comes home give him this purse with these hundred guineas. I cannot stay, I have business. Good day to you. *(Exits.)*
TRUFFALDINO. And a good day to you, sir! He never even told me to which of my masters I was to give it.

Enter FLORINDO.

FLORINDO. Well, did you find Pasquale?
TRUFFALDINO. No, Sir, I didn't find Pasqual', but I found a gentleman who gave me a purse with a hundred guineas in it.

FLORINDO. A hundred guineas? What for?

TRUFFALDINO. Tell me truly, sir, were you expecting money from anyone?

FLORINDO. Yes; I had presented a letter of credit to a merchant.

TRUFFALDINO. Then this money will be for you.

FLORINDO. What did he say when he gave it to you?

TRUFFALDINO. He told me to give it to my master.

FLORINDO. Then of course it is mine. Am I not your master? What doubt could you have?

TRUFFALDINO. *(Aside.)* Yes, but what about t'other one?

FLORINDO. And you do not know who gave you the money?

TRUFFALDINO. No, sir; I think I have seen his face somewhere, but I don't remember exactly.

FLORINDO. It will have been the merchant to whom I had a letter.

TRUFFALDINO. Yes, of course, sir.

FLORINDO. You won't forget Pasquale.

TRUFFALDINO. I'll find him after dinner.

FLORINDO. Then let us go and order our meal. *(Goes into the inn.)*

TRUFFALDINO. We will. Lucky I made no mistake this time. I've given the purse to the right one. *(Goes into the inn.)*

SCENE III
A Room in the House of Pantalone.

PANTALONE and CLARICE.

PANTALONE. That's the long and short of it; Signor Federigo is to be your husband. I have given my word and I am not to be cozened.

CLARICE. You have my obedience, sir; but I beseech you, this is tyranny.

PANTALONE. When Signor Federigo first asked for your hand, I told you; you never replied that you did not wish to marry him. You should have spoken then; now it is too late.

CLARICE. My fear of you, sir, and my respect, made me dumb.

PANTALONE. Then your fear and respect should do the same now.

CLARICE. Indeed I cannot marry him, sir.

PANTALONE. No? And why not?

CLARICE. Nothing shall induce me to marry Federigo.

PANTALONE. You dislike him so much?

CLARICE. He is odious in my eyes.

PANTALONE. And supposing I were to show you how you might begin to like him a little?

CLARICE. What do you mean, sir?

PANTALONE. Put Signor Silvio out of your mind, and you will soon like Federigo well enough.

CLARICE. Silvio is too firmly stamped upon my heart; and your own approval, sir, has rooted him there the more securely.

PANTALONE. *(Aside.)* In some ways I am sorry for her. *(To CLARICE.)* You have got to make a virtue of necessity.

CLARICE. My heart is not capable of so great an effort.

PANTALONE. Come, come; you shall!

Enter SMERALDINA.

SMERALDINA. Sir, Signor Federigo is here and desires to speak with you.

PANTALONE. Tell him to come in; I am at his service.

CLARICE. *(Weeping.)* Alas! what torture!

SMERALDINA. What is it, madam? you are weeping? Truly you do wrong. Have you not noticed how handsome Signor Federigo is? If I had such luck, I would not cry; no, I would laugh with the whole of my mouth. *(Exits.)*

PANTALONE. There, there, my child; you must not be seen crying.

CLARICE. But if I feel my heart bursting!

Enter BEATRICE in man's dress.

BEATRICE. My respects to Signor Pantalone.

PANTALONE. Your servant, sir. Did you receive a purse with a hundred guineas in it?

BEATRICE. No.

PANTALONE. But I gave it to your servant just now. You told me he was a trustworthy man.

BEATRICE. Yes, indeed; there is no danger. I did not see him. He will give me the money when I come home again. *(Aside to PANTALONE.)* What ails Signora Clarice that she is weeping?

PANTALONE. *(Aside to BEATRICE.)* Dear Signor Federigo, you must have pity on her. The news of your death was the cause of this trouble. I hope it will pass away in time.

BEATRICE. *(To PANTALONE.)* Do me a kindness, Signor Pantalone, and leave me alone with her a moment, to see if I cannot obtain a kind word from her.

PANTALONE. With pleasure, sir. I will go, and come back again. *(To CLARICE.)* My child, stay here, I will be back directly. You must entertain your promised husband awhile. *(Softly to CLARICE.)* Now, be careful. *(Exits.)*

BEATRICE. Signora Clarice, I beg you—

CLARICE. Stand away, and do not dare to importune me.

BEATRICE. So severe with him who is your destined husband?

CLARICE. They may drag me by force to the altar, but you will have only my hand, never my heart.

BEATRICE. You disdain me, but I hope to appease you.

CLARICE. I shall abhor you to all eternity.

BEATRICE. If you knew me, you would not say so.

CLARICE. I know you well enough as the destroyer of my happiness.

BEATRICE. But I have the means of comforting you.

CLARICE. You deceive yourself; there is no one but Silvio who can comfort me.

BEATRICE. 'Tis true, I cannot give you the same comfort as your Silvio might, but I can at least contribute to your happiness.

CLARICE. I think it is already enough, sir, that though I speak to you as harshly as possible, you should continue to torture me.

BEATRICE. *(Aside.)* Poor girl! I can't bear to see her suffer.

CLARICE. *(Aside.)* I'm so angry, I don't care how rude I am.

BEATRICE. Signora Clarice, I have a secret to tell you.

CLARICE. I make no promise to keep it; you had better not tell it me.

BEATRICE. Your austerity deprives me of the means to make you happy.

CLARICE. You can never make me anything but miserable.

BEATRICE. You are wrong, and to convince you I will speak plainly. You have no desire for me, I have no use for you. You have promised your hand to another, I to another have pledged my heart.

CLARICE. Oh! Now you begin to please me.

BEATRICE. Did I not tell you that I knew how to comfort you?

CLARICE. Ah, I fear you would deceive me.

BEATRICE. Nay, madam, I speak in all sincerity and if you promise me that discretion which you refused me just now, I will confide to you a secret, which will ensure your peace of mind.

CLARICE. I vow I will observe the strictest silence.

BEATRICE. I am not Federigo Rasponi, but his sister Beatrice.

CLARICE. What! I am amazed. You a woman?

BEATRICE. I am indeed. Imagine my feelings when I claimed you as my bride!

CLARICE. And what news have you of your brother?

BEATRICE. He died indeed by the sword. A lover of mine was thought to have killed him, and 'tis he whom I am seeking now in these clothes. I beseech you by all the holy laws of friendship and of love not to betray me.

CLARICE. Won't you let me tell Silvio?

BEATRICE. No; on the contrary I forbid you absolutely.

CLARICE. Well, I will say nothing.

BEATRICE. Remember I count upon you.

CLARICE. You have my promise. I will be silent.

BEATRICE. Now, I hope, you will treat me more kindly.

CLARICE. I will be your friend indeed; and if I can be of service to you, dispose of me.

BEATRICE. I too swear eternal friendship to you. Give me your hand.

CLARICE. I don't quite like to—

BEATRICE. Are you afraid I am not a woman after all? I will give you proof positive.

CLARICE. It all seems just like a dream.

BEATRICE. Yes. 'Tis a strange business.

CLARICE. 'Tis indeed fantastic.

BEATRICE. Come, I must be going. Let us embrace in sign of honest friendship and loyalty.

CLARICE. There! I doubt you no longer.

Enter PANTALONE.

PANTALONE. Well done, well done; I congratulate you. *(To CLARICE.)* My child, you have been very quick in adapting yourself.

BEATRICE. Did I not tell you, Signor Pantalone, that I should win her round?

PANTALONE. Magnificent! You have done more in four minutes than I should have done in four years.

CLARICE. *(Aside.)* Now I am in a worse tangle than ever.

PANTALONE. *(To CLARICE.)* Then we will have the wedding at once.

CLARICE. Pray do not be in too much haste, sir.

PANTALONE. What? Holding hands on the sly and kissing and then in no haste about it? No, no, I don't want you to get yourself into trouble. You shall be married to-morrow.

BEATRICE. Signor Pantalone, 'twill be necessary first of all to arrange the settlement and to go into our accounts.

PANTALONE. We will do all that. These things can be done in two hours.

CLARICE. Sir, I beseech you—

PANTALONE. Madam, I am going straight away to say a word to Signor Silvio.

CLARICE. For the love of heaven do not anger him.

PANTALONE. What, what? do you want two husbands?

CLARICE. Not exactly—but—

PANTALONE. But me no buts. 'Tis all settled. Your servant, sir. *(Going.)*

BEATRICE. Listen, sir—

PANTALONE. You are husband and wife. *(Going.)*

CLARICE. You had better—

PANTALONE. We will talk about it this evening. *(Exits.)*

CLARICE. Oh, Signora Beatrice, 'tis worse than it was before!

END OF ACT I

ACT II

SCENE I
The courtyard of Pantalone's house.

SILVIO and DOCTOR LOMBARDI.

SILVIO. Sir, I entreat you to leave me alone.

LOMBARDI. Stay, answer me.

SILVIO. I am beside myself.

LOMBARDI. What are you doing in the courtyard of Signor Pantalone?

SILVIO. I intend either that he should keep his word that he has given me, or that he should render me account for this intolerable insult.

LOMBARDI. But you cannot do this in Pantalone's own house. You are a fool to let yourself be so transported with anger.

SILVIO. A man who behaves so abominably deserves no consideration.

LOMBARDI. True; but that is no reason why you should be so rash. Leave it to me, my dear boy, leave it to me; let me talk to him; may be I can bring him to reason and make him see where his duty lies. Go away somewhere and wait for me; leave this courtyard; do not let us make a scene. I will wait for Signor Pantalone.

SILVIO. But sir, I—

LOMBARDI. But sir, I will have you obey me.

SILVIO. I obey you, sir. I will go. Speak to him. I wait for you at the apothecary's. But if Signor Pantalone persists, he will have to settle with me. *(Exits.)*

LOMBARDI. Poor boy, I am sorry for him. Signor Pantalone ought never to have led him on so far before he was quite certain that the fellow from Turin was dead. I must see him quietly; I must not let my temper get the better of me.

Enter PANTALONE.

PANTALONE. *(Aside.)* What is the Doctor doing in my house?

LOMBARDI. Oh Signor Pantalone, your servant.

PANTALONE. Your servant, Doctor. I was just going to look

for you and your son.

LOMBARDI. Indeed? Good! I suppose you were coming to give us your assurance that Signora Clarice is to be Silvio's wife.

PANTALONE. *(Much embarrassed.)* Well, the fact is, I was coming to tell you—

LOMBARDI. No, no; there is no need for explanations. You have my sympathy in a very awkward situation. But we are old friends and we will let bygones be bygones.

PANTALONE. *(Still hesitating.)* Yes, of course, in view of the promise made to Signor Federigo—

LOMBARDI. He took you by surprise, and you had no time for reflection; you did not think of the affront you were giving to our family.

PANTALONE. You can hardly talk of an affront, when a previous contract—

LOMBARDI. I know what you are going to say. It seemed at first sight out of the question that your promise to the Turin gentleman could be repudiated, because it was a formal contract. But that was a contract merely between you and him; whereas ours is confirmed by the girl herself.

PANTALONE. Very true, but—

LOMBARDI. And as you know, in matrimonial cases, Consensus, et non concubitus, facit virum.

PANTALONE. I am no Latin scholar; but I must tell you—

LOMBARDI. And girls must not be sacrificed.

PANTALONE. Have you anything more to say?

LOMBARDI. I have nothing more to say.

PANTALONE. Have you finished?

LOMBARDI. I have finished.

PANTALONE. May I speak?

LOMBARDI. You may.

PANTALONE. My dear Doctor, with all your learning—

LOMBARDI. As regards the dowry, we can easily arrange matters. A little more or a little less, I will make no difficulties.

PANTALONE. I must begin all over again. Will you allow me to speak?

LOMBARDI. With pleasure.

PANTALONE. I must tell you; I have the greatest respect for your legal learning, but in this case it does not apply.

LOMBARDI. And you mean to tell me that this other marriage is to take place?

PANTALONE. For my part I have given my word and I cannot go back upon it. My daughter is content; what impediment can there be? I was just coming to look for you or Signor Silvio, to tell you this. I am extremely sorry, but I see no help for it.

LOMBARDI. I am not surprised at your daughter's behaviour. But I am surprised at yours, sir, at your treating me in this disgraceful way. If you were not perfectly certain about the death of Signor Federigo, you had no business to enter into an engagement with my son; and having entered into an engagement with him, you are bound to maintain that engagement whatever it may cost you. The news of Federigo's death was quite sufficient to justify, even to Federigo, your new intention; he could have no right to reproach you, still less to demand any sort of compensation. The marriage which was contracted this morning between Signora Clarice and my son coram testibus cannot be dissolved by a mere word given by you to another party. If I were to listen to my son I should insist upon the annulment of the new contract and compel your daughter to marry him; but I should be ashamed to receive into my house so disreputable a daughter-in-law, the daughter of a man who breaks his word as you do. Signor Pantalone, you have done me an injury, you have done an injury to the house of Lombardi. The time will come, when you will have to pay for it; yes, sir, the time will come—omnia tempus habent. *(Exits.)*

PANTALONE. You may go to the devil for all I care. I don't care a fig, I'm not afraid of you. The Rasponis are worth a hundred of the Lombardis. An only son, and as rich as he is—you won't find that every day. It has got to be.

Enter SILVIO.

SILVIO. *(Aside.)* 'Tis all very fine for my father to talk. Let him keep his temper who can.

PANTALONE. *(Seeing SILVIO, aside.)* Here comes the other.

SILVIO. *(Rudely.)* Your servant, sir.

PANTALONE. Yours to command, sir. *(Aside.)* He is smoking.

SILVIO. I have just heard something from my father; am I to believe that it is true?

PANTALONE. If your father said it, it must certainly be true.

SILVIO. Then the marriage is settled between Signora Clarice and Signor Federigo?

PANTALONE. Yes, sir, settled and concluded.

SILVIO. I am amazed that you should have the face to tell me so. You are a man of no reputation, you are no gentleman.

PANTALONE. What is all this? Is that the way you speak to a man of my age?

SILVIO. I don't care how old you are; I have a mind to run you straight through the body.

PANTALONE. I am not a frog, sir, to be spitted. Do you come into my house to make all this turmoil?

SILVIO. Come outside then.

PANTALONE. I am surprised at you, sir.

SILVIO. Come on, if you are a man of honour.

PANTALONE. I am accustomed to be treated with respect.

SILVIO. You are a low fellow, a coward and a villain.

PANTALONE. You are a most impertinent young man.

SILVIO. I swear to Heaven—*(Lays his hand to his sword.)*

PANTALONE. Help! murder! *(Draws a pistol.)*

Enter BEATRICE with a drawn sword.

BEATRICE. *(To PANTALONE)* I am here to defend you.

PANTALONE. My dear son-in-law, I thank you.

SILVIO. *(To BEATRICE.)* You are just the man I want to fight.

BEATRICE. *(Aside.)* I am in for it now.

SILVIO. *(To BEATRICE.)* Come on, sir.

PANTALONE. *(Frightened.)* My dear son-in-law—

BEATRICE. It is not the first time that I have been in danger. *(To SILVIO.)* I am not afraid of you. *(Presents sword.)*

PANTALONE. Help! help!

PANTALONE runs towards the street. BEATRICE and SILVIO fight. SILVIO falls and drops his sword. BEATRICE holds her point to his heart. Enter CLARICE.

CLARICE. *(To BEATRICE.)* Stop, stop!

BEATRICE. Fair Clarice, at your request I give Silvio his life, and in consideration of my mercy, I beg you to remember your oath. *(Exits.)*

CLARICE. Dear Silvio, are you hurt?

SILVIO. Dear Silvio! faithless deceiver! Dear Silvio! to a lover disdained, to a betrayed husband!

CLARICE. No, Silvio, I do not deserve your reproaches. I love you, I adore you, I am indeed faithful.

SILVIO. Oh lying jade! Faithful to me, forsooth! You call that fidelity, to plight your troth to another?

CLARICE. I never did so, nor will I ever. I will die rather than desert you.

SILVIO. I heard just now that you had given your oath.

CLARICE. My oath does not bind me to marry him.

SILVIO. Then what did you swear?

CLARICE. Dear Silvio, have mercy on me; I cannot tell you.

SILVIO. Why not?

CLARICE. Because I am sworn to silence.

SILVIO. That proves your guilt.

CLARICE. No, I am innocent.

SILVIO. Innocent people have no secrets.

CLARICE. Indeed I should be guilty if I spoke.

SILVIO. And to whom have you sworn this silence?

CLARICE. To Federigo.

SILVIO. And you will observe it so jealously?

CLARICE. I will observe it, rather than be a perjuress.

SILVIO. And you tell me you do not love him? He's a fool that believes you. I do not believe you, cruel, deceiver! Begone from my sight!

CLARICE. If I did not love you, I should not have run hither in all haste to save your life.

SILVIO. Then I loathe my life, if I must owe it to one so ungrateful.

CLARICE. I love you with all my heart.

SILVIO. I abhor you with all my soul.

CLARICE. I will die, if you are not to be appeased.

SILVIO. I would sooner see you dead than unfaithful.

CLARICE. Then you shall have that satisfaction.

He picks up his sword.

SILVIO. Yes, that sword should revenge my wrongs.
CLARICE. Are you so cruel to your Clarice?
SILVIO. 'Twas you that taught me cruelty.
CLARICE. Then you desire my death?
SILVIO. I know not what I desire.
CLARICE. I do. *(Points the sword at her breast.)*

SMERALDINA enters.

SMERALDINA. Stop, stop! What on earth are you doing? *(Takes the sword away from CLARICE.)* And you, you dog, you would have let her die? *(To SILVIO.)* Have you the heart of a tiger, of a hyena, of a devil? Look at you, you're a pretty little fellow, that expects ladies to disembowel themselves for you! You are much too kind to him, madam. He doesn't want you any more, I suppose? The man that doesn't want you doesn't deserve you. Let this murderer go to the devil; and you come along with me. There's no shortage of men; I'll promise to find you a dozen before evening.

She throws down the sword, SILVIO picks it up.

CLARICE. *(Weeping.)* Ungrateful! Can it be that my death should not cost you a single sigh? But I shall die, and that of grief. I shall die, and you will be content. But one day you will know that I am innocent, and then, when it is too late, you will be sorry you did not believe me, you will weep for my misfortune and for your own barbarous cruelty. *(Exits.)*
SMERALDINA. Here's something I really don't understand. Here's a girl on the point of killing herself, and you sit there looking on, just as if you were at a play.
SILVIO. Nonsense, woman! Do you suppose she really meant to kill herself?
SMERALDINA. How should I know? I know that if I had not arrived in time, she would have been gone, poor thing.
SILVIO. The point was nowhere near her heart.

SMERALDINA. Did you ever hear such a lie? It was just ready to pierce her.

SILVIO. You women always invent things.

SMERALDINA. We should indeed, if we were like you. It's as the old saw says; we get the kicks and you the halfpence. They say women are unfaithful, but men are committing infidelities all day long. People talk about the women, and they never say a word about the men. We get all the blame, and you are allowed to do as you please. Do you know why? Because 'tis the men who have made the laws. If the women had made them, things would be just the other way. If I were a queen, I'd make every man who was unfaithful carry a branch of a tree in his hand, and I know all the towns would look like forests. *(Exits.)*

SILVIO. Clarice faithless! Clarice a traitress! Her pretence at suicide was a trick to deceive me, to move my compassion. But though fate made me fall before my rival, I will never give up the thought of revenge. That wretch shall die, and my ungrateful Clarice shall see her lover wallowing in his own gore. *(Exits.)*

SCENE II
A room in the inn, with a door at each side and two doors at the back, facing the audience.

TRUFFALDINO solus.

TRUFFALDINO. Just my luck! Two masters, and neither of them comes home to dinner. 'Tis two o'clock, and not one to be seen. Sure enough they will both come at the same time, and I shall be in a mess; I shall not be able to wait on both together, and the whole thing will be found out. Hush, here comes one. All the better.

FLORINDO enters.

FLORINDO. Well, did you find that fellow Pasquale?

TRUFFALDINO. Didn't we say, sir, that I was to look for him after dinner?

FLORINDO. I am impatient to see him.

TRUFFALDINO. You should have come to dinner a little sooner.

FLORINDO. *(Aside.)* I can find no way of making certain whether Beatrice is here.

TRUFFALDINO. You told me to go and order dinner, and then you go out. The dinner will have been spoiled.

FLORINDO. I don't want to eat anything. *(Aside.)* I shall go to the Post; I must go myself; then perhaps I shall find out something.

TRUFFALDINO. You know, sir, at Venice you must eat; if you do not, you will fall sick.

FLORINDO. I must go out; I have important business. If I come back to dinner, well and good; if not, I shall eat in the evening. You can get yourself some food, if you like.

TRUFFALDINO. Very good, sir; just as you please, sir; you're the master.

FLORINDO. This money is heavy; here, put it in my trunk. There is the key. *(Gives Truffaldino the purse and his keys.)*

TRUFFALDINO. Certainly, sir; I'll bring the key back at once.

FLORINDO. No, no, you can give it me later. I can't stop. If I do not come back to dinner come to the Piazza; I can't rest till you have found Pasquale. *(Exits.)*

TRUFFALDINO. Well, any way, he said I could get myself some food; we are agreed about that. If he won't eat his dinner, he can leave it. My complexion was not made for fasting. I'll just put away this purse, and then—

Enter BEATRICE.

BEATRICE. Oh, Truffaldino!

TRUFFALDINO. *(Aside.)* The devil!

BEATRICE. Did Signor Pantalone dei Bisognosi give you a purse of a hundred ducats?

TRUFFALDINO. Yes, sir, indeed he did.

BEATRICE. Then why did you not give it to me?

TRUFFALDINO. Was it meant for your honour?

BEATRICE. Was it meant for me? What did he say when he gave you the purse?

TRUFFALDINO. He told me I was to give it to my master.

BEATRICE. Well, and who is your master?

TRUFFALDINO. Your honour.

BEATRICE. Then why do you ask if the purse is mine?

TRUFFALDINO. Then it will be yours.

BEATRICE. Where is it?

TRUFFALDINO. Here, sir. *(Gives BEATRICE the purse.)*

BEATRICE. Is the money all there?

TRUFFALDINO. I never touched it, sir.

BEATRICE. *(Aside.)* I shall count it.

TRUFFALDINO. *(Aside.)* I made a mistake over the purse; but that puts it straight. I wonder what the other gentleman will say? Oh well, if the money wasn't his, he'll say nothing at all.

BEATRICE. Is the landlord in?

TRUFFALDINO. Yes, sir.

BEATRICE. Tell him I shall have a friend to dinner with me, and he must get it ready as soon as ever he can.

TRUFFALDINO. What do you want for dinner, sir? How many dishes?

BEATRICE. Oh, Signor Pantalone dei Bisognosi is not a man who expects a great deal. Tell him to give us five or six dishes; something good.

TRUFFALDINO. You leave it all to me, sir?

BEATRICE. Yes, you order it, do the best you can. I am going to fetch the gentleman, he is not far off. See that all is ready by the time we come back. *(Going.)*

TRUFFALDINO. You shall see how they serve you here.

BEATRICE. Look! Take this paper; put it in my trunk. Be careful with it; 'tis a bill of exchange for four thousand crowns.

TRUFFALDINO. Be sure of it, sir, I'll put it away at once.

BEATRICE. See that everything is ready. *(Aside.)* Poor old Signor Pantalone—I gave him a terrible fright! I must cheer him up a little. *(Exits.)*

TRUFFALDINO. Now's the time to do myself proud. 'Tis the first time this master of mine has told me to order him a dinner. I'll show him I am a man of good taste. I'll just put away this paper and then—no, I'll put it away afterwards, I must not waste time. Ho there! is nobody at home? *(Calling into the inn.)* Call master Brighella, tell him I want to talk to him. *(Returning.)* Now with a really good dinner 'tis not the having such and such dishes, but the way it is served. A properly laid table is worth more than a mountain of dishes.

Enter BRIGHELLA.

BRIGHELLA. What is it, Si'or Truffaldin'? What can I do for you?

TRUFFALDINO. My master has got a gentleman to dine with him. He wants a good dinner, and that quickly. Have you got enough in the kitchen?

BRIGHELLA. I always have plenty of everything. In half an hour I can put on any sort of dinner you like.

TRUFFALDINO. Very well, then. Tell me what you can give us.

BRIGHELLA. For two persons, we will have two courses of four dishes each. Will that do?

TRUFFALDINO. He said five or six dishes—better say six or eight. That will do. What will you give us?

BRIGHELLA. For the first course I shall give you soup, fried, boiled, and a fricandeau.

TRUFFALDINO. Three of the dishes I know, but I do not know the last.

BRIGHELLA. 'Tis a French dish—a ragout—very tasty indeed.

TRUFFALDINO. Very well, that will do for the first course; now the second.

BRIGHELLA. For the second course the roast, the salad, a meat pie and a pudding.

TRUFFALDINO. There's another dish I don't know; what's this "pudding"?

BRIGHELLA. I said a pudding, an English dish—very good indeed.

TRUFFALDINO. Good, that will do; but how are we to arrange the table?

BRIGHELLA. Oh, that's easy enough. The waiter will see to that.

TRUFFALDINO. No, my good friend, laying the table is a very important matter; that's the first thing about a dinner, to have the table laid properly.

BRIGHELLA. Well, you might put the soup here, the fried there, there the boiled and here the fricandeau. *(Makes an imaginary arrangement.)*

TRUFFALDINO. I don't like that. Don't you put something in the middle?

BRIGHELLA. Then we should want five dishes.

TRUFFALDINO. Good, then let us have five.

BRIGHELLA. We can put the gravy in the middle.

TRUFFALDINO. No, no, friend, you know nothing about laying a table; you can't put the gravy in the middle; soup always goes in the middle.

BRIGHELLA. Then the meat on one side, and the gravy on the other.

TRUFFALDINO. Lord, lord, that won't do at all. You innkeepers may know how to cook, but you have no idea of butlering. Now I'll show you. *(Kneels down on one knee and points to the floor.)* Suppose this is the table. Now you look how we arrange the five dishes. Like this: here in the middle the soup. *(He tears off a piece of the bill of exchange and puts it on the floor to represent a dish.)* Now the boiled meat. *(Same business.)* Here we put the fried opposite *(Same business.)*, here the gravy and here that—what-d'ye-call-it. There now! Won't that look fine?

BRIGHELLA. H'm, 'twill do; but you have put the gravy too far away from the meat.

TRUFFALDINO. Very well, we must see if we can't put it a little nearer.

Enter BEATRICE and PANTALONE.

BEATRICE. What are you doing on your knees?

TRUFFALDINO. *(Stands up.)* I was just planning how to have the table laid.

BEATRICE. What is that paper?

TRUFFALDINO. *(Aside.)* The devil! the letter that he gave me!

BEATRICE. That is my bill of exchange.

TRUFFALDINO. I am very sorry, sir; I will stick it together again.

BEATRICE. You rascal! Is that the way you look after my things? things of such value too! You deserve a good thrashing. What say you, Signor Pantalone? did you ever see such a piece of folly?

PANTALONE. To tell the truth, I cannot help laughing. 'Twould be a serious matter if it could not be mended, but I will write you out another and then all will be in order.

BEATRICE. But just think if the bill had been made out not here but in some place a long way off. *(To TRUFFALDINO.)* You ignorant fool!

TRUFFALDINO. This has all come about because Brighella did not know how to lay a table.

BRIGHELLA. He finds fault with everything I do.

TRUFFALDINO. I am a man that knows his business.

BEATRICE. *(To TRUFFALDINO.)* Go away.

TRUFFALDINO. Things must be done properly.

BEATRICE. Be off, I tell you.

TRUFFALDINO. In the matter of pantry work I won't give way to the first butler in the land. *(Exits.)*

BRIGHELLA. I don't understand that fellow; sometimes he is a knave and sometimes a fool.

BEATRICE. This tomfoolery is all put on. Well, is dinner ready?

BRIGHELLA. If you will have five dishes to each course, 'twill take a little time.

PANTALONE. What's this about courses of five dishes? We'll take pot luck—a risotto, a couple of other dishes, and I shall be most obliged to you. My tastes are simple.

BEATRICE. *(To BRIGHELLA.)* You hear that? That will do nicely.

BRIGHELLA. Very good, sir; but will you please to tell me if there might be anything you would particularly fancy?

PANTALONE. I should like some rissoles if you have them; my teeth are not very good nowadays.

BEATRICE. You hear? Rissoles.

BRIGHELLA. Very good, sir. If you will sit down here for a moment, gentlemen, dinner will be ready directly.

BEATRICE. Tell Truffaldino to come and wait on us.

BRIGHELLA. I'll tell him, sir. *(Exits.)*

BEATRICE. Signor Pantalone, I fear you will indeed have to be content with pot luck.

PANTALONE. My dear sir, I am overcome with all the

attention you show me; in fact you are doing for me what I ought to be doing for you. But you see, I have that girl of mine at home, and until everything is finally settled it would not be proper for you to be together. So I accept your kind hospitality to raise my spirits a little; indeed I still feel quite upset. Had it not been for you, that young scoundrel would have done for me.

BEATRICE. I am glad that I arrived in time.

The WAITERS enter from the kitchen and carry glasses, wine, bread, etc. into the room where BEATRICE and PANTALONE are to dine.

PANTALONE. They are very quick about their business here.

BEATRICE. Brighella is a smart fellow. He was servant to a great nobleman at Turin, and still wears his livery.

PANTALONE. There's a very good tavern on the other side of the Grand Canal opposite the Rialto where you can eat very well; I have often been there with various good friends of mine, very sound men too; I often think of that place. They had some wonderful Burgundy wine there too—'twas a wine for the gods.

BEATRICE. There's nothing one enjoys more than good wine in good company.

PANTALONE. Good company! Ah, if you had known them! That was good company! Good honest fellows, with many a good story to tell. God bless them. Seven or eight of them there were, and there wasn't the like of them in all the world.

The WAITERS come out of the room and return to the kitchen.

BEATRICE. You often had a merry time with these gentlemen, eh?

PANTALONE. And I hope I may live to have many more.

TRUFFALDINO enters carrying the soup-tureen.

TRUFFALDINO. *(To BEATRICE.)* Dinner is ready for you in that room, sir.

BEATRICE. Go and put the soup on the table.

TRUFFALDINO. *(Makes a bow.)* After you, sir.

PANTALONE. A queer fellow, that servant of yours. *(Goes in.)*

BEATRICE. *(To TRUFFALDINO.)* I want less wit and more attention. *(Goes in.)*

TRUFFALDINO. Call that a dinner! one dish at a time! They have money to spend, but they get nothing good for it. I wonder if this soup is worth eating; I'll try it. *(Takes a spoon out of his pocket and tastes the soup.)* I always carry my weapons about. Not bad; it might be worse. *(Goes into the room with the soup.)*

The FIRST WAITER enters with a dish.

FIRST WAITER: When is that man coming to take the dishes?

TRUFFALDINO. *(Re-entering.)* Here I am, friend. What have you got for me?

FIRST WAITER: Here's the boiled meat. There's another dish to follow. *(Exits.)*

TRUFFALDINO. Mutton? or veal? Mutton, I think. Let's taste it. *(Tastes.)* No, 'tis neither mutton nor veal; 'tis lamb, and very good too. *(Goes towards Beatrice's room.)*

Enter FLORINDO.

FLORINDO. Where are you going?

TRUFFALDINO. Oh dear, oh dear! *(Aside.)*

FLORINDO. What are you doing with that dish?

TRUFFALDINO. I was just putting it on the table, sir.

FLORINDO. For whom?

TRUFFALDINO. For you, sir.

FLORINDO. Why do you serve dinner before I come in?

TRUFFALDINO. I saw you from the window. *(Aside.)* I must find some excuse.

FLORINDO. And you begin with boiled meat instead of soup?

TRUFFALDINO. You must know, sir, at Venice soup is always taken last.

FLORINDO. I have other habits. I want my soup. Take that back to the kitchen.

TRUFFALDINO. Yes, sir, as you wish, sir.

FLORINDO. Make haste; afterwards I want to have a nap.

TRUFFALDINO. Yes, sir. *(Makes as if going to the kitchen.)*
FLORINDO. *(Aside.)* Shall I never find Beatrice again?

FLORINDO goes into the other room—as soon as he is in TRUFFALDINO quickly takes the dish in to Beatrice. The FIRST WAITER enters with another dish. FLORINDO calls from his room.

FLORINDO. Truffaldino! Truffaldino! am I always to be kept waiting?
TRUFFALDINO. *(Coming out of Beatrice's room.)* Coming, sir. *(To the FIRST WAITER.)* Quick, go and lay the table in that other room, the other gentleman has arrived; bring the soup at once.
FIRST WAITER. Directly. *(Exits.)*
TRUFFALDINO. What may this dish be? Thus must be the "fricandeau." *(Tastes it.)* That's good, upon my word. *(Takes it in to Beatrice.)*

The WAITERS enter and carry glasses, wine, bread, etc. into Florindo's room.

TRUFFALDINO. *(To the WAITERS.)* Good lads, that's right. *(Aside.)* They are as lively as kittens. Well, if I can manage to wait at table on two masters at once, 'twill be a great accomplishment indeed.

The WAITERS come back out of Florindo's room and go towards the kitchen.

TRUFFALDINO. Hurry up, lads, the soup!
FIRST WAITER. You look after your own table; we'll take care of this one.

The WAITERS exit.

TRUFFALDINO. I want to look after both, if I can.

Re-enter the FIRST WAITER with Florindo's soup.

TRUFFALDINO. Here, give me that; I'll take it. Go and get the stuff for the other room. *(Takes soup from the FIRST WAITER and carries it into Florindo's room.)*

FIRST WAITER. That's a strange fellow. He wants to wait on every one. Let him. They will have to give me my tip all the same.

TRUFFALDINO comes out of Florindo's room.

BEATRICE. *(Calling from her room.)* Truffaldino!
FIRST WAITER. *(To TRUFFALDINO.)* Your master's calling.
TRUFFALDINO. Coming, sir. *(Goes into Beatrice's room.)*

The SECOND WAITER brings the boiled meat for Florindo. TRUFFALDINO brings the dirty plates out of Beatrice's room.

TRUFFALDINO. Here, give it me.

The SECOND WAITER exits.

FLORINDO. *(Calls.)* Truffaldino!
TRUFFALDINO. *(Wishes to take the meat from the WAITER.)* Give it me.
FIRST WAITER. No, I'm taking this.
TRUFFALDINO. Didn't you hear him call for me? *(Takes meat from him and carries it in to Florindo.)*
FIRST WAITER. Well, that's fine! He wants to do everything.

The SECOND WAITER brings in a dish of rissoles, gives it to the FIRST WAITER and exits.

I would take this in myself, but I don't want to have words with that fellow.

Re-enter TRUFFALDINO from Florindo's room with dirty plates.

Here, master Jack-of-all-trades; take these rissoles to your master.
TRUFFALDINO. *(Takes dish.)* Rissoles?

FIRST WAITER. Yes, the rissoles he ordered. *(Exits.)*

TRUFFALDINO. Oh, fine! To which of them are they to go? Now which the devil of my two masters can have ordered them? If I go to the kitchen and ask, they'll begin to suspect; if I make a mistake and carry them to the one who didn't order them, then the other will ask for them and I shall be found out. I know what I'll do; I'll divide them on two plates, take half to each, and then I shall see who ordered them. *(Takes plates and divides the rissoles.)* That's four and that's four. There's one over. Who's to have that? We mustn't cause ill-feeling; I'll eat that one myself. *(Eats it.)* Now. We'll take the rissoles to this gentleman.

TRUFFALDINO puts one plate of rissoles on the floor and takes the other in to Beatrice. The FIRST WAITER enters with an English Pudding.

FIRST WAITER. Truffaldino!

TRUFFALDINO. *(Comes out of Beatrice's room.)* Coming!

FIRST WAITER. Take this pudding—

TRUFFALDINO. Wait a moment, I'm coming. *(Takes the other dish of rissoles and is going to Florindo's room.)*

FIRST WAITER. That's not right, the rissoles belong there.

TRUFFALDINO. I know they do, sir; I have carried them there; and my master sends these four as a courtesy to this gentleman. *(Goes into Florindo's room.)*

FIRST WAITER. I see, they know each other—friends, you might say? They might as well have dined together.

TRUFFALDINO. *(Re-entering.)* And what's this affair?

FIRST WAITER. That's an English Pudding.

TRUFFALDINO. Who is it for?

FIRST WAITER. For your master. *(Exits.)*

TRUFFALDINO. What the devil is this "pudding"? It smells delicious, and looks like polenta. Oh! if it is polenta, that would be good indeed. I'll taste it. *(Brings a fork out of his pocket and tries the pudding.)* It's not polenta, but it's very like it. *(Eats.)* Much better than polenta. *(Goes on eating.)*

BEATRICE. *(Calling.)* Truffaldino!

TRUFFALDINO. *(With mouth full.)* Coming, sir.

FLORINDO. *(Calling.)* Truffaldino!

TRUFFALDINO. *(With mouth full.)* Coming, sir. *(To himself.)* Oh what wonderful stuff! just another mouthful and then I'll go. *(Goes on eating.)*

BEATRICE comes out of her room, sees TRUFFALDINO eating, and kicks him.

BEATRICE. You come and wait on me. *(She goes back to her room.)* Truffaldino!
TRUFFALDINO. Coming!

TRUFFALDINO puts the pudding on the floor and goes into Beatrice's room. FLORINDO comes out of his.

FLORINDO. *(Calling.)* Truffaldino! Where the devil is he?

TRUFFALDINO comes out of Beatrice's room.

TRUFFALDINO. *(Seeing FLORINDO.)* Here, sir.
FLORINDO. What are you doing? Where have you been?
TRUFFALDINO. I just went to fetch the next course, sir.
FLORINDO. Is there anything more to eat?
TRUFFALDINO. I'll go and see.
FLORINDO. Make haste, I tell you, because I want to have a nap afterwards. *(Goes back into his room.)*
TRUFFALDINO. Very good, sir. *(Calling.)* Waiter, is there anything more to come? *(Aside.)* I'll put this pudding aside for myself. *(Hides it.)*

The FIRST WAITER enters with a dish.

FIRST WAITER. Here's the roast.
TRUFFALDINO. *(Takes the roast.)* Quick, the dessert!
FIRST WAITER. Lord, what a fluster! In a minute. *(Exits.)*
TRUFFALDINO. I'll take the roast to this gentleman. *(Takes it to Florindo.)*

Re-enter the FIRST WAITER.

FIRST WAITER. *(With a plate of fruit.)* Here's the dessert; where are you?

TRUFFALDINO. *(Re-entering from Florindo's room.)* Here.

FIRST WAITER. *(Gives him the fruit.)* There. Anything more?

TRUFFALDINO. Wait. *(Takes the dessert to Beatrice.)*

FIRST WAITER. He jumps about here and there like the devil himself.

TRUFFALDINO. *(Re-entering.)* That will do. Nobody wants any more.

FIRST WAITER. I'm glad to hear it.

TRUFFALDINO. And now lay the table for me.

FIRST WAITER. In a moment. *(Exits.)*

TRUFFALDINO. Now for my pudding! Hurrah! I've got through it all, they are all content, they want nothing more, they've had a very good dinner. I have waited at table on two masters at once, and neither knew of the other. But if I have waited for two, now I am going to eat for four.

SCENE III
A street with Brighella's inn.

Enter SMERALDINA.

SMERALDINA. A very proper sort of young lady my mistress is! To send me all alone with a letter to a tavern, a young girl like me! Waiting on a woman in love is a sad business. This young lady of mine does a thousand crazy things, and what I cannot understand is this—if she is so much in love with Signor Silvio as to be ready to disembowel herself for him, why does she send letters to another gentleman? One
for summer and one for winter, I suppose! Well, there it is! I am not going inside that tavern. I'll call; somebody will come out. Hey there! anyone at home?

The FIRST WAITER comes out of the inn.

FIRST WAITER. Now, young woman, what do you want?

SMERALDINA. *(Aside.)* I feel thoroughly ashamed. *(To the WAITER.)* Tell me—a certain Signor Federigo Rasponi lodges here, does he not?

FIRST WAITER. Yes, indeed. He has just this moment finished dinner.

SMERALDINA. I have something to say to him.

FIRST WAITER. A message? You can come inside.

SMERALDINA. And what sort of a girl do you take me for? I am the waiting-maid of the lady he is to marry.

FIRST WAITER. Well then, pray step this way.

SMERALDINA. Oh, but I don't like to go in there.

FIRST WAITER. Do you expect me to bring him out into the street for you? That would not be at all the right thing; more especially as he has Signor Pantalone dei Bisognosi with him.

SMERALDINA. What, my master? Worse and worse! I'll not come in.

FIRST WAITER. I can send his servant, if you like.

SMERALDINA. The little dark man?

FIRST WAITER. Exactly so.

SMERALDINA. Yes, do send him.

FIRST WAITER. *(Aside.)* I understand. She fancies the little dark man, and is ashamed to come inside. She is not ashamed to be seen with him in the middle of the street. *(Goes in.)*

SMERALDINA. If the master sees me, whatever shall I say? I'll tell him I came to look for him; that will do nicely. I'm never short of an answer.

TRUFFALDINO enters with a bottle in his hand, a glass and a napkin.

TRUFFALDINO. Who sent for me?

SMERALDINA. I did, sir. I ask pardon if I have troubled you.

TRUFFALDINO. Not a bit of it. I am here to receive your commands.

SMERALDINA. I fear I must have taken you from your dinner.

TRUFFALDINO. I was having dinner, but I can go back to it.

SMERALDINA. I am truly sorry.

TRUFFALDINO. I am delighted. The fact is, I have had my bellyful, and your bright eyes are just the right thing to make me digest it.

SMERALDINA. *(Aside.)* Very gallant!

TRUFFALDINO. I'll just set down this bottle, and then I'm with you, my dear.

SMERALDINA. *(Aside.)* He called me "my dear"! *(To TRUFFALDINO.)* My mistress sends this letter to Signor Federigo Rasponi. I do not like to come into the tavern, so I thought I might put you to this trouble, as you are his man.

TRUFFALDINO. I'll take it with pleasure; but first, you must know that I have a message for you.

SMERALDINA. From whom?

TRUFFALDINO. From a very honest man. Tell me, are you acquainted with one Truffaldin' Battocchio?

SMERALDINA. I think I have heard him spoken of, but I am not sure. *(Aside.)* It must be himself.

TRUFFALDINO. He's a good-looking man; short, thickset, with plenty of wit to his talk. Understands butlering too—

SMERALDINA. I don't know him from Adam.

TRUFFALDINO. Yes, you do; and what's more, he's in love with you.

SMERALDINA. Oh! you are making fun of me.

TRUFFALDINO. And if he could only have just a little hope that his affections were returned, he would make himself known.

SMERALDINA. Well, sir, if I were to see him, and he took my fancy, it might possibly be that I should return his affection.

TRUFFALDINO. Shall I show him to you?

SMERALDINA. I should like to see him.

TRUFFALDINO. Just a moment. *(Goes into the inn.)*

SMERALDINA. Then 'tis not he.

TRUFFALDINO comes out of the inn, makes low bows to SMERALDINA, passes close to her, sighs, and goes back into the inn.

SMERALDINA. I do not understand this play-acting.

TRUFFALDINO. *(Re-entering.)* Did you see him?

SMERALDINA. See whom?

TRUFFALDINO. The man who is in love with your beauty.

SMERALDINA. I saw no one but you.

TRUFFALDINO. *(Sighs.)* Well!

SMERALDINA. Is it you, then, who profess to be in love with me?

TRUFFALDINO. It is. *(Sighs.)*

SMERALDINA. Why did you not say so before?

TRUFFALDINO. Because I am rather shy.

SMERALDINA. *(Aside.)* He would make a stone fall in love with him.

TRUFFALDINO. Well, and what do you say?

SMERALDINA. I say—

TRUFFALDINO. Come, tell me.

SMERALDINA. Oh—I am rather shy too.

TRUFFALDINO. Then if we were joined up, 'twould be a marriage of two people who are rather shy.

SMERALDINA. I must say, you are just my fancy.

TRUFFALDINO. Are you a maid?

SMERALDINA. Need you ask?

TRUFFALDINO. I suppose that means "certainly not".

SMERALDINA. On the contrary, it means "certainly I am".

TRUFFALDINO. I am a bachelor too.

SMERALDINA. I could have been married fifty times, but I never found the man I really fancied.

TRUFFALDINO. Do you think there is any hope for me?

SMERALDINA. Well—to tell the truth—really—I must say— there's a—something about you—No, I won't say another word.

TRUFFALDINO. If somebody wanted to marry you, what would he have to do?

SMERALDINA. I have neither father nor mother. He would have to speak to my master, or to my mistress.

TRUFFALDINO. And if I speak to them, what will they say?

SMERALDINA. They will say, that if I am content—

TRUFFALDINO. And what will you say?

SMERALDINA. I shall say—that if they are content too—

TRUFFALDINO. That will do. We shall all be content. Give me the letter and when I bring you back the answer, we will have a talk.

SMERALDINA. Here's the letter.

TRUFFALDINO. Do you know what is in it?

SMERALDINA. No—if you only knew how curious I am to know!

TRUFFALDINO. I hope it is not a disdainful letter, or I shall get my face spoiled.

SMERALDINA. Who knows? It can't be a love-letter.

TRUFFALDINO. I don't want to get into trouble. If I don't know what is in the letter, I am not going to take it.

SMERALDINA. We could open it—but how are we to seal it again?

TRUFFALDINO. Leave it to me; sealing letters is just my job. No one will ever know anything.

SMERALDINA. Then let us open it.

TRUFFALDINO. Can you read?

SMERALDINA. A little. But you can read well, I'm sure.

TRUFFALDINO. Yes, I too can read just a little.

SMERALDINA. Then let us hear.

TRUFFALDINO. We must open it cleanly. *(Tears off a piece.)*

SMERALDINA. Oh! what have you done?

TRUFFALDINO. Nothing. I've a secret way to mend it. Here it is, open.

SMERALDINA. Quick, read it.

TRUFFALDINO. You read it. You will know your young lady's handwriting better than I do.

SMERALDINA. *(Looking at the letter.)* Really, I can't make out a word.

TRUFFALDINO. *(Same business.)* Nor I neither.

SMERALDINA. Then what was the good of opening it?

TRUFFALDINO. *(Takes the letter.)* Wait; let me think; I can make out some of it.

SMERALDINA. Oh I know some of the letters too.

TRUFFALDINO. Let us try one by one. Isn't that an M?

SMERALDINA. No! that's an R!

TRUFFALDINO. Between R and M there is very little difference.

SMERALDINA. Ri, ri, o. No, no; keep quiet; I think it is an M—Mi, mi, o,—mio!

TRUFFALDINO. It's not mio, it's mia.

SMERALDINA. But it is, there's the hook—

TRUFFALDINO. That proves it is mia.

BEATRICE comes out of the inn with PANTALONE.

PANTALONE. *(To SMERALDINA.)* What are you doing here?

SMERALDINA. *(Frightened.)* Nothing, sir; I came to look for you.

PANTALONE. *(To SMERALDINA.)* What do you want with me?

SMERALDINA. The mistress wants you, sir.

BEATRICE. *(To TRUFFALDINO.)* What is this paper?

TRUFFALDINO. *(Frightened.)* Nothing, just a bit of paper—

BEATRICE. Let me see.

TRUFFALDINO. *(Gives paper, trembling.)* Yes, sir.

BEATRICE. What? This is a letter addressed to me. Villain, will you open all my letters?

TRUFFALDINO. I know nothing about it, sir—

BEATRICE. Look, Signor Pantalone, here is a letter from Signora Clarice, in which she tells me of Silvio's insane jealousy—and this rascal has the impudence to open it!

PANTALONE. *(To SMERALDINA.)* And you helped him to do so?

SMERALDINA. I know nothing about it, sir.

BEATRICE. Who opened this letter?

TRUFFALDINO. Not I.

SMERALDINA. Nor I.

PANTALONE. Well, who brought it?

SMERALDINA. Truffaldino brought it to his master.

TRUFFALDINO. And Smeraldina brought it to Truffaldino.

SMERALDINA. *(Aside.)* Sneak! I don't like you any more.

PANTALONE. You meddlesome little hussy, so you are the cause of all this trouble are you? I've a good mind to smack your face.

SMERALDINA. I've never had my face smacked by any man; I'm surprised at you.

PANTALONE. *(Coming near her.)* Is that the way you answer me?

SMERALDINA. You won't catch me. You're too rheumatic, you can't run. *(Exits running.)*

PANTALONE. You saucy minx, I'll show you if I can run; I'll catch you. *(Runs after her.)*

TRUFFALDINO. *(Aside.)* If I only knew how to get out of this!

BEATRICE. *(Looking at the letter, aside.)* Poor Clarice! she is in despair over Silvio's jealousy; 'twill be best for me to discover myself and set her mind at rest.

TRUFFALDINO. *(Tries to steal away quietly.)* I don't think he is looking. I'll try to get away.

BEATRICE. Where are you off to?

TRUFFALDINO. Nowhere. *(Stops.)*

BEATRICE. Why did you open this letter?

TRUFFALDINO. It was Smeraldina; I had nothing to do with it.

BEATRICE. Smeraldina, forsooth! You did it, you rascal. One and one make two. That's the second letter of mine you have opened to-day. Come here.

TRUFFALDINO. *(Approaching timidly.)* Oh for mercy's sake, sir—

BEATRICE. Come here, I say.

TRUFFALDINO. *(Same business.)* Oh for the love of Heaven—

BEATRICE takes the stick which TRUFFALDINO has at his flank (i.e. Harlequin's wooden sword or baton) and beats him well, she standing with her back to the inn. FLORINDO appears at the window and sees the beating.

FLORINDO. What's this? beating my servant? *(Leaves window.)*

TRUFFALDINO. Stop, stop, sir, for pity's sake.

BEATRICE. Take that, rascal, and learn to open my letters. *(Throws stick down on the ground, and exits to the street.)*

TRUFFALDINO. *(After BEATRICE has gone.)* My blood! My body! Is that the way to treat a man of my sort? Beat a man like me? If a servant is no good, you can send him away, but you don't beat him.

FLORINDO comes out unseen by TRUFFALDINO.

FLORINDO. What's that?

TRUFFALDINO. *(Seeing FLORINDO.)* Oh! I said people had no business to beat other people's servants like that. This is an insult to my master. *(Looking towards direction of Beatrice's exit.)*

FLORINDO. Yes, 'tis an affront put upon me. Who was it gave you a thrashing?

TRUFFALDINO. I couldn't say, sir; I do not know him.

FLORINDO. Why did he thrash you?

TRUFFALDINO. Because I—I spat on his shoe.

FLORINDO. And you let yourself be beaten like that? did nothing? made no attempt to defend yourself? And you expose your master to insult, with perhaps serious consequences? Ass! fool! poltroon! *(Picks up the stick)* Since you enjoy being thrashed, I'll give you your pleasure, I'll thrash you myself as well. *(Thrashes him and exits into the inn.)*

TRUFFALDINO. Well, there's no mistake about my being the servant of two masters. They have both paid me my wages. *(Exits into the inn.)*

END OF ACT II

ACT III

SCENE I
A Room in Brighella's Inn.

TRUFFALDINO solus.

TRUFFALDINO. I don't care that for my beating! I have eaten well, I've dined well and this evening I shall sup still better; and as long as I can serve two masters, there's this at least, that I draw double wages. And now what's to be done? Master number one is out of doors, master number two is fast asleep; why, it's just the moment to give those clothes an airing—take them out of the trunks and see if there's anything wants doing. Here are the keys. This room will do nicely. I'll get the trunks out and make a proper job of it. I must have some one to help me though. *(Calls.)* Waiter!

The WAITERS enter.

FIRST WAITER. What do you want?

TRUFFALDINO. I want you to lend a hand to bring some trunks out of those rooms, to give the clothes an airing.

FIRST WAITER. *(To the SECOND WAITER.)* Go and help him.

TRUFFALDINO. *(To the SECOND WAITER.)* Come along, and I'll give you a good handful of what my masters gave me.

TRUFFALDINO and the SECOND WAITER go into Beatrice's room.

FIRST WAITER. He looks like a rare good servant—quick, ready and most attentive; but I'll warrant he has his faults somewhere. I've been a servant myself and I know the ropes. Nobody does anything just for love. Whatever they do, either they are robbing their master or they are throwing dust in his eyes.

TRUFFALDINO comes out of the room with the SECOND WAITER carrying a trunk.

TRUFFALDINO. Gently! let's put it down here. *(They put the trunk in the middle of the room.)* Now let's fetch the other. But quietly, for my master is in there asleep.

TRUFFALDINO and the SECOND WAITER go into Florindo's room.

FIRST WAITER. Either he's a real first-rate fellow, or he's a real knave; I never saw anybody wait on two gentlemen at once like that. I shall just keep my eyes open; maybe, under the pretence of waiting on two gentlemen at once, he means to rob them both.

TRUFFALDINO and the SECOND WAITER re-enter with the other trunk.

TRUFFALDINO. And we'll put this one here. *(They put it down a little way off from the other.) (To the SECOND WAITER.)* There! You can run along now, if you like, I don't want anything more.

FIRST WAITER. *(To the SECOND WAITER.)* Go on; off with you to the kitchen. *(To TRUFFALDINO, as the SECOND WAITER exits.)* Can I help you?

TRUFFALDINO. No, thank you; I can do my work myself.

FIRST WAITER. I must say, you are a giant for work; it's a marvel to me how you get through it all. *(Exits.)*

TRUFFALDINO. Now I'm going to do my work properly, in peace and quiet with no one to worry me. *(Takes a key out of his pocket.)* Now which key is this, I wonder? which trunk does it fit? Let's try. *(Opens one trunk.)* I guessed right at once. I'm the cleverest man on earth. And this other will open t'other trunk. *(Takes out second key and opens the second trunk.)* Now they are both open. Let's take everything out. *(He takes all the clothes out of both trunks and puts them on the table. In each trunk there must be a black suit, books and papers, and anything else ad lib.)* I'll just see if there is anything in the pockets. You never know, sometimes they leave biscuits or sweets in them. *(Searches the pockets of Beatrice's suit and finds a portrait.)* My word, what a pretty picture? There's a handsome man! Who can it be? A queer thing, I seem to know him, but yet I can't remember. He is just the least little bit like my other master; but no, he never wears clothes like that, nor that wig neither.

FLORINDO calls from his room.

FLORINDO. Truffaldino!

TRUFFALDINO. Oh plague take him! he has woken up. If the devil tempts him to come out and he sees this other trunk, he'll want to know—quick, quick—I'll lock it up and say I don't know whose it is. *(Begins putting clothes in again.)*

FLORINDO. *(Calling.)* Truffaldino!

TRUFFALDINO. Coming, sir! *(Aside.)* I must put these things away first. But I can't remember which trunk this coat came from, nor these papers neither.

FLORINDO. *(Calling.)* Come here, I say; or must I fetch a stick to you?

TRUFFALDINO. In a minute, sir. *(Aside.)* Quick, before he comes! I'll put all straight when he goes out. *(Stuffs the things into the trunks anyhow and locks them.)*

FLORINDO comes out in a dressing-gown.

FLORINDO. What the devil are you doing?

TRUFFALDINO. Pray, sir, didn't you tell me to give your clothes an airing? I was just about to do it here.

FLORINDO. And this other trunk, whose is that?

TRUFFALDINO. I couldn't say, sir; 'twill belong to some other gentleman.

FLORINDO. Give me my black coat.

TRUFFALDINO. Very good, sir. *(Opens Florindo's trunk and gives him the black suit.)*

FLORINDO takes off his dressing-gown with TRUFFALDINO's help and puts on the black coat; then puts his hand into the pockets and finds the portrait.

FLORINDO. *(Much surprised.)* What is this?

TRUFFALDINO. *(Aside.)* Oh Lord, I've made a mistake. I ought to have put it into the other gentleman's pocket. 'Tis the colour made me go wrong.

FLORINDO. *(Aside.)* Heavens! There can be no mistake. This is my own portrait; the one I gave to my beloved Beatrice. *(To TRUFFALDINO.)* Tell me, how ever did this portrait come to be in the pocket of my coat? It wasn't there before.

TRUFFALDINO. *(Aside.)* Now what's the answer to that? I don't know. Let me think—

FLORINDO. Come on, out with it, answer me. How did this portrait come to be in my pocket?

TRUFFALDINO. Sir, be kind and forgive me for taking a liberty. The portrait belongs to me, and I hid it there for safety, for fear I might lose it.

FLORINDO. How did you come by this portrait?

TRUFFALDINO. My master left it to me.

FLORINDO. Left it to you?

TRUFFALDINO. Yes, sir; I had a master who died, and he left me a few trifles which I sold, all except this portrait, sir.

FLORINDO. Great heavens! and how long is it since this master of yours died?

TRUFFALDINO. 'Twill be just about a week ago, sir. *(Aside.)* I say the first thing that comes into my head.

FLORINDO. What was your master's name?

TRUFFALDINO. I do not know, sir; he lived incognito.

FLORINDO. Incognito? How long were you in his service?

TRUFFALDINO. Only a short time, sir; ten or twelve days.

FLORINDO. *(Aside.)* Heavens! More and more do I fear that it was Beatrice. She escaped in man's dress; she concealed her name—Oh wretched me, if it be true!

TRUFFALDINO. *(Aside.)* As he believes it all, I may as well go on with the fairy-tale.

FLORINDO. *(Despairingly.)* Tell me, was your master young?

TRUFFALDINO. Yes, sir, quite a young gentleman.

FLORINDO. Clean shaven?

TRUFFALDINO. Clean shaven, sir.

FLORINDO. *(Aside, with a sigh.)* 'Twas she, doubtless.

TRUFFALDINO. *(Aside.)* I hope I'm not in for another thrashing.

FLORINDO. At least, you know where your late master came from?

TRUFFALDINO. I did know, sir, but I can't now call it to mind.

FLORINDO. Was he from Turin?

TRUFFALDINO. Turin it was, sir.

FLORINDO. *(Aside.)* Every word he speaks is a sword-thrust in my heart. *(To TRUFFALDINO.)* Tell me again; this young gentleman from Turin, is he really dead?

TRUFFALDINO. He is dead indeed, sir.

FLORINDO. Of what did he die?

TRUFFALDINO. He met with an accident, and that was the end of him. *(Aside.)* That seems to be the best way out.

FLORINDO. Where was he buried?

TRUFFALDINO. *(Aside.)* I wasn't ready for that one. *(To FLORINDO.)* He wasn't buried, sir.

FLORINDO. What!

TRUFFALDINO. No, sir, another servant from the same place got permission to have him put into a coffin and sent home, sir.

FLORINDO. And was it, by any chance, the same servant who got you to fetch his letters for him from the Post this morning?

TRUFFALDINO. Exactly so, sir; it was Pasqual'.

FLORINDO. *(Aside.)* Then all hope is lost. Beatrice is dead. Unhappy Beatrice! the discomforts of the journey and the tortures of her heart must have killed her. Oh! I can no longer endure the agony of my grief! *(Exits into his room.)*

TRUFFALDINO. That portrait has touched him in the guts. He must have known the gentleman. Well, I had better take the trunks back to the rooms again, or I shall be in for more trouble of the same sort. Oh! dear! here comes my other master.

Enter BEATRICE and PANTALONE.

BEATRICE. I assure you, Signor Pantalone, the last consignment of mirrors and wax candles has been put down twice over.

PANTALONE. Maybe my young men have made a mistake. We will go through the books again, and then we shall find out exactly how things stand.

BEATRICE. I too have a list copied from my own books. We will compare them. Perhaps that may decide the point either in your favour or mine. Truffaldino!

TRUFFALDINO. Here, sir.

BEATRICE. Have you the key of my trunk?

TRUFFALDINO. Yes, sir; here it is.

BEATRICE. Why have you brought my trunk in here?

TRUFFALDINO. To air your clothes, sir.

BEATRICE. Have you aired them?

TRUFFALDINO. I have, sir.

BEATRICE. Open the trunk and give me—whose is that other trunk?

TRUFFALDINO. It belongs to another gentleman who has just come.

BEATRICE. Give me the memorandum book which you will find there.

TRUFFALDINO. Yes, sir. *(Aside.)* The Lord help me this time! *(Opens trunk and looks for the book.)*

PANTALONE. As I say, they may have made a mistake; of course, if there is a mistake, you will not have to pay.

BEATRICE. We may find that all is in order; we shall see.

TRUFFALDINO. Is this the book, sir? *(Holding out a book to BEATRICE.)*

BEATRICE. I expect so.

He takes the book without looking carefully and opens it.

No, this is not it—Whose is this book?

TRUFFALDINO. *(Aside.)* I've done it now!

BEATRICE. *(Aside.)* These are two letters which I wrote to Florindo. Alas! These notes, these accounts belong to him. I tremble, I am in a cold sweat, I know not where I am.

PANTALONE. What ails you, Signor Federigo? Are you unwell?

BEATRICE. 'Tis nothing. *(Aside to TRUFFALDINO.)* Truffaldino, how did this book come to be in my trunk? It is not mine.

TRUFFALDINO. I hardly know, sir—

BEATRICE. Come, out with it—tell me the truth.

TRUFFALDINO. I ask your pardon for the liberty I took, sir, putting the book into your trunk. It belongs to me, and I put it there for safety. *(Aside.)* That was a good enough story for the other gentleman, I hope 'twill do for this one too.

BEATRICE. The book is your own, you say, and yet you gave it to me instead of mine, without noticing?

TRUFFALDINO. *(Aside.)* He's much too clever. *(To BEATRICE.)* I'll tell you, sir; I have only had the book a very short time, so I did not recognise it at once.

BEATRICE. And how came you by this book?

TRUFFALDINO. I was in service with a gentleman at Venice, and he died and left the book to me.

BEATRICE. How long ago?

TRUFFALDINO. I don't remember exactly—ten or twelve days.

BEATRICE. How can that be, when I met you at Verona?

TRUFFALDINO. I had just come away from Venice on account of my poor master's death.

BEATRICE. *(Aside.)* Alas for me! *(To TRUFFALDINO.)* Your master—was his name—Florindo?

TRUFFALDINO. Yes, sir; Florindo.

BEATRICE. And his family name Aretusi?

TRUFFALDINO. That was it, sir; Aretusi.

BEATRICE. And you are sure he is dead?

TRUFFALDINO. As sure as I stand here.

BEATRICE. Of what did he die? Where was he buried?

TRUFFALDINO. He tumbled into the canal and was drowned and never seen again.

BEATRICE. Oh wretched that I am! Florindo is dead, my beloved is dead; my one and only hope is dead. All is lost. Love's stratagems are fruitless! I leave my home, I leave my relatives, I dress as a man, I confront danger, I hazard my very life, all for Florindo—and Florindo is dead. Unhappy Beatrice! Was the loss of my brother so little to me, that Fate must make me lose my lover as well? Oh! Grief overwhelms me, I can no longer bear the light of day. My adored one, my beloved, I will follow you to the tomb.

(Exits into her room, raving.)

PANTALONE. *(Astonished.)* Truffaldino!

TRUFFALDINO. Si'or Pantalon'?

PANTALONE. A woman!

TRUFFALDINO. A female!

PANTALONE. Most extraordinary!

TRUFFALDINO. Who'd have thought it?

PANTALONE. I'm struck all of a heap.

TRUFFALDINO. You might knock me down with a feather.

PANTALONE. I shall go straight home and tell my daughter. *(Exits.)*

TRUFFALDINO. It seems I am not the servant of two masters but of a master and a mistress. *(Exits.)*

SCENE II
A Street.

Enter Doctor LOMBARDI meeting PANTALONE.

LOMBARDI. *(Aside.)* This doddering old villain Pantalone sticks in my gizzard. The more I think about him, the more I abominate him.

PANTALONE. *(Cheerfully.)* Good day, my dear Doctor, your servant.

LOMBARDI. I am surprised that you have the effrontery to address me.

PANTALONE. I have news for you. Do you know—

LOMBARDI. You are going to tell me that the marriage has already been performed? I care not a fig if it has.

PANTALONE. The whole story is untrue. Let me speak, plague take you.

LOMBARDI. Speak on then, pox on you.

PANTALONE. *(Aside.)* I should like to give him a good doctoring with my fists. *(To LOMBARDI.)* My daughter shall marry your son whenever you please.

LOMBARDI. I am vastly obliged to you. Pray do not put yourself to inconvenience. My son is not prepared to stomach that, sir. You may give her to the Turin gentleman.

PANTALONE. If you knew who the Turin gentleman is, you would say differently.

LOMBARDI. He may be who he will. Your daughter has been seen with him, et hoc sufficit.

PANTALONE. But 'tis not true that he is—

LOMBARDI. I will not hear another word.

PANTALONE. If you won't hear me, 'twill be the worse for you.

LOMBARDI. We shall see for whom it will be the worse.

PANTALONE. My daughter is a girl of unblemished reputation, and—

LOMBARDI. The devil take you.

PANTALONE. The devil take you, sir.

LOMBARDI. You disreputable old villain! *(Exits.)*

PANTALONE. Damn you! He is more like a beast than a man. Why, how could I ever tell him that the man was a woman? Not a bit of it, he wouldn't let me speak. But here comes that young lout of a son of his; now I shall be in for more impertinence.

Enter SILVIO.

SILVIO. *(Aside.)* There is Pantalone. I should like to run a sword through his paunch.

PANTALONE. Signor Silvio, if you will give me leave, I should like to give you a piece of good news, if you will condescend to allow me to speak, and not behave like that windmill of a father of yours.

SILVIO. What have you to say to me? Pray speak, sir.

PANTALONE. You must know, sir, that the marriage of my daughter to Signor Federigo has come to nothing.

SILVIO. Indeed? Do not deceive me.

PANTALONE. 'Tis true indeed, and if you are still of your former mind, my daughter is ready to give you her hand.

SILVIO. Oh heavens! You bring me back from death to life.

PANTALONE. *(Aside.)* Well, well, he is not quite such a bear as his father.

SILVIO. But heavens! how can I clasp to my bosom her who has for so long been the bride of another?

PANTALONE. To cut a long story short, Federigo Rasponi has turned into Beatrice his sister.

SILVIO. What? I do not understand you.

PANTALONE. Then you are very thick-headed. The person whom we thought to be Federigo has been discovered to be Beatrice.

SILVIO. Dressed as a man?

PANTALONE. Dressed as a man.

SILVIO. At last I understand.

PANTALONE. About time you did.

SILVIO. How did it happen? Tell me.

PANTALONE. Let us go to my house. My daughter knows nothing of it. I need only tell the story once to satisfy you both.

SILVIO. I will come, sir; and I most humbly beg your forgiveness, for having allowed myself to be transported by passion—

PANTALONE. 'Twas a mere nothing; I appreciate your feelings. I know what love is. Now, my dear boy, come along with me. *(Going.)*

SILVIO. *(Aside.)* Who is happier than I am? what heart could be more contented? (*SILVIO and PANTALONE exit.*)

SCENE III
A Room in Brighella's Inn.

BEATRICE and FLORINDO come out of their rooms simultaneously. Each holds a sword or dagger and is on the point of committing suicide. BRIGHELLA is restraining BEATRICE and the FIRST WAITER restraining FLORINDO. They all come forward in such a way that BEATRICE and FLORINDO are unaware of each other's presence.

BRIGHELLA. *(Seizing BEATRICE's hand.)* Stop, stop!

BEATRICE. *(Trying to break loose.)* For pity's sake, let me go.

FIRST WAITER. *(Holding FLORINDO.)* This is madness.

FLORINDO. *(Breaks away from the WAITER.)* Go to the devil.

BEATRICE. *(Breaking away from BRIGHELLA.)* You shall not hinder me.

Both come forward, determined to kill themselves, they see each other, recognise each other and stand dazed.

FLORINDO. What do I see?
BEATRICE. Florindo!
FLORINDO. Beatrice!
BEATRICE. Are you alive?
FLORINDO. Are you too living?
BEATRICE. Oh destiny!

FLORINDO. Oh my adored one!

They drop their weapons and embrace.

BRIGHELLA. *(Jokingly to the WAITER.)* You had better mop up the blood; we don't want a mess here. *(Exits.)*

FIRST WAITER. *(Aside.)* Any way I'll pick up the weapons and I shan't give them back again. *(Picks up the daggers and exits.)*

FLORINDO. What brought you to attempt such an act of madness?

BEATRICE. The false news of your death.

FLORINDO. Who told you that I was dead?

BEATRICE. My servant.

FLORINDO. And mine gave me to believe that you were dead; and I too, carried away by the same agony of grief, intended to take my life.

BEATRICE. It was this book caused me to believe the story.

FLORINDO. That book was in my trunk. How came it into your hands? Ah, now I know. By the same means doubtless as the portrait I found in my coat pocket. Here it is. The one I gave you at Turin.

BEATRICE. Those rascally servants of ours—Heaven only knows what they have been up to.

FLORINDO. Where are they, I wonder?

BEATRICE. Nowhere to be seen.

FLORINDO. Let us find them and confront them. *(Calling.)* Ho there! Is nobody there?

Enter BRIGHELLA.

BRIGHELLA. Did you call, sir?

FLORINDO. Where are our servants?

BRIGHELLA. I don't know, sir. Shall I send to look for them?

FLORINDO. Find them at once if you can and send them to us here.

BRIGHELLA. For myself I only know one of them; I will ask the waiters, they will know them both. I congratulate you, sir, and madam, on having made such a pleasant end of yourselves; if you want to get yourselves buried, you must try some other establishment; there is no room here. Your servant, madam and sir. *(Exits.)*

FLORINDO. Then you too are lodged in this inn?

BEATRICE. I arrived this morning.

FLORINDO. I too this morning. And yet we never saw each other.

BEATRICE. Fate has been pleased to torture us a little.

FLORINDO. Tell me: your brother Federigo—is he dead?

BEATRICE. Have you any doubt? He died on the spot.

FLORINDO. I was told he was alive and here in Venice.

BEATRICE. It was I who travelled in his name and in these clothes to follow—

FLORINDO. To follow me—I know, my dearest; I read it in a letter from your servant at Turin.

BEATRICE. How came it into your hands?

FLORINDO. My servant gave it me by mistake and seeing it was addressed to you, I could not help opening it.

BEATRICE. I suppose a lover's curiosity is always legitimate.

FLORINDO. But where are these servants of ours? Ah! *(Sees TRUFFALDINO approaching.)* Here is one.

BEATRICE. He looks like the worse knave of the two.

FLORINDO. I think you are not far wrong.

Enter TRUFFALDINO brought in by force by BRIGHELLA and the FIRST WAITER.

FLORINDO. Come here, come here, don't be frightened.

BEATRICE. We shall do you no harm.

TRUFFALDINO. *(Aside.)* H'm, I still remember the thrashing.

BRIGHELLA. We have found this one; if we can find the other, we will bring him.

FLORINDO. Yes, we must have them both here together.

BRIGHELLA. *(Aside to the WAITER.)* Do you know the other?

FIRST WAITER. *(To BRIGHELLA.)* Not I.

BRIGHELLA. We'll ask in the kitchen. Someone there will know him.

FIRST WAITER. If he had been there, I should have known him too.

The FIRST WAITER and BRIGHELLA exit.

FLORINDO. *(To TRUFFALDINO.)* Come now, tell us what happened about that changing of the portrait and the book, and why you and that other rascal conspired to drive us distracted.

TRUFFALDINO. *(Signs to both with his finger to keep silence.)* Hush! *(To FLORINDO.)* Pray, sir, a word with you in private. *(To BEATRICE, just as he turns to speak to FLORINDO.)* I will tell you everything directly. *(To FLORINDO.)* You must know, sir, I am not to blame for any thing that has happened; it's all Pasqual's fault, the servant of that lady there *(Cautiously pointing at BEATRICE.)* It was he mixed up the things, and put into one trunk what belonged to the other, without my knowledge. The poor man begged and prayed me to take the blame, for fear his master should send him away, and as I am a kind-hearted fellow that would let himself be drawn and quartered for his friends, I made up all these stories to see if I could help him. I never dreamt it was a portrait of you or that you would be so much upset at hearing of the death of the owner. Now I have told you the whole truth, sir, as an honest man and a faithful servant.

BEATRICE. *(Aside.)* 'Tis a very long story he is telling. I am curious to know what the mystery is about.

FLORINDO. *(Aside to TRUFFALDINO.)* Then the man who got you to fetch that letter from the Post was the servant of Signora Beatrice?

TRUFFALDINO. *(Aside to FLORINDO.)* Yes, sir, that was Pasqual'.

FLORINDO. Then why conceal from me a fact I so urgently desired to know?

TRUFFALDINO. He begged me not to tell anyone, sir.

FLORINDO. Who?

TRUFFALDINO. Pasqual'.

FLORINDO. Why didn't you obey your master?

TRUFFALDINO. For the love of Pasqual'.

FLORINDO. You and Pasquale deserve a sound thrashing together.

TRUFFALDINO. *(Aside to himself.)* In that case I should get both.

BEATRICE. Have you not yet finished this long cross-examination?

FLORINDO. This fellow has been telling me—

TRUFFALDINO. *(Aside to FLORINDO.)* For the love of heaven, your honour, do not say it was Pasqual'. I'd rather you told the lady it was me. You can give me a beating if you like, but don't, don't let any trouble come to Pasqual'.

FLORINDO. *(Aside to TRUFFALDINO.)* Are you so devoted a friend to Pasquale?

TRUFFALDINO. I love him as if he were my own brother. Now I am going to the lady, and I am going to tell her that it was all my fault; she may scold me as she pleases and do what she will to me, but I will protect Pasqual'. *(TRUFFALDINO moves towards BEATRICE.)*

FLORINDO. Well, *(Aside.)* He's certainly a very loyal and affectionate character.

TRUFFALDINO. *(To BEATRICE.)* Here I am, madam.

BEATRICE. *(Aside to TRUFFALDINO.)* What is all this long story you've been telling Signor Florindo?

TRUFFALDINO. *(Aside to BEATRICE.)* You must know, madam, that that gentleman has a servant called Pasqual'; he is the most arrant noddy in the world; it was he made all that mess of things; but because the poor man was afraid his master would send him away, I made up all that story about the book and the master who was dead and drowned, and all the rest of it. And just now I've been telling Si'or Florindo that I was the cause of it all.

BEATRICE. But why accuse yourself of faults which you have never committed?

TRUFFALDINO. Madam, 'tis all for the love I bear Pasqual'.

FLORINDO. *(Aside.)* This seems a very long business.

TRUFFALDINO. *(To BEATRICE, as before.)* Dear madam, I beg of you, don't get him into trouble.

BEATRICE. Whom?

TRUFFALDINO. Pasqual'.

BEATRICE. Pasquale and you are a pretty pair of rascals.

TRUFFALDINO. *(Aside to himself.)* I fear I'm the only one.

FLORINDO. Come. That's enough. Signora Beatrice, our servants certainly deserve to be punished; but in consideration of our own great happiness, we surely may forgive what is past.

BEATRICE. True; but your servant—

TRUFFALDINO. *(Aside to BEATRICE.)* For the love of Heaven don't mention Pasqual'.

BEATRICE. *(To FLORINDO.)* Well, I must go and call upon Signor Pantalone dei Bisognosi. Will you accompany me?

FLORINDO. I would do so with pleasure, but I have to wait here and see my banker. I will come later, if you are in haste.

BEATRICE. I am, I must go at once. I shall expect you at Signor Pantalone's; and shall stay there till you come.

FLORINDO. I don't know where he lives.

TRUFFALDINO. I know, sir, I'll show you the way.

BEATRICE. Very well, and now I must go to my room and tidy myself up.

TRUFFALDINO. *(Aside to BEATRICE.)* Very good, madam; I am at your service directly.

BEATRICE. Dear Florindo! what torments have I not endured for love of you! *(She goes into her room.)*

FLORINDO. Mine have been no less.

TRUFFALDINO. Sir, Pasqual' is not here, and Si'ora Beatrice has no one to help her to dress. Will you give me leave to wait upon her instead of Pasqual'?

FLORINDO. Yes, by all means. Wait upon her with diligence; I am delighted.

TRUFFALDINO. *(Aside.)* For invention, for promptness and for intrigue I will challenge the Attorney-General. *(Goes into Beatrice's room.)*

FLORINDO. What strange things have happened in the course of this one day! Tears, lamentations and anguish, and then at last consolation and happiness. From tears to laughter is a happy step, which makes us forget our agonies, but when we pass from pleasure to pain the change is even yet more acutely perceptible.

Re-enter BEATRICE followed by TRUFFALDINO.

BEATRICE. Here I am, have I not been quick?

FLORINDO. When will you change that dress?

BEATRICE. Do I not look well in it?

FLORINDO. I long to see you in a woman's dress. Your

beauties ought not to be so completely disguised.

BEATRICE. Well, I shall expect you at Signor Pantalone's; make Truffaldino show you the way.

FLORINDO. I must wait for the banker; if he does not come soon another time will do.

BEATRICE. Show me your love in your anxiety to attend me. *(About to go.)*

TRUFFALDINO. *(Aside to BEATRICE.)* Do you wish me to stay and wait upon this gentleman?

BEATRICE. Yes, you will show him the way to Signor Pantalone's.

TRUFFALDINO. Yes, madam, certainly, as Pasqual' is not here.

BEATRICE. Wait upon him, I shall be pleased indeed. *(Aside to herself.)* I love him more than my very self. *(Exits.)*

TRUFFALDINO. The fellow's nowhere to be seen. His master wants to dress, and he goes out on his own and is nowhere to be found.

FLORINDO. Of whom are you speaking?

TRUFFALDINO. Of Pasqual'. I love him, he is a good friend of mine, but he's a lazy dog. Now I am a servant worth two.

FLORINDO. Come and dress my wig. The banker will be here directly.

TRUFFALDINO. Please your honour, I hear your honour has to go to Si'or Pantalon's.

FLORINDO. Yes, what then?

TRUFFALDINO. I want to ask a favour of you.

FLORINDO. Well, you deserve it after all you have done.

TRUFFALDINO. If there has been any trouble, you know, sir, 'tis all the fault of Pasqual'.

FLORINDO. But where on earth is this cursed Pasquale? Can't one see him?

TRUFFALDINO. He'll come, the knave. And so, sir, I want to ask you this favour.

FLORINDO. What do you want?

TRUFFALDINO. You see, sir, I'm in love too.

FLORINDO. In love?

TRUFFALDINO. Yes, sir, and my young woman is maidservant to Si'or Pantalon'; and it would be very kind if your honour—

FLORINDO. How do I come into it?

TRUFFALDINO. I won't say, sir, that you come into it; but I being your servant, you might say a word for me to Si'or Pantalon'.

FLORINDO. We must see first whether the girl wants you.

TRUFFALDINO. The girl wants me, no mistake. All I want is a word to Si'or Pantalon'. I beg you, sir, of your charity.

FLORINDO. Certainly I will speak for you, but how can you keep a wife?

TRUFFALDINO. I shall do what I can. I shall ask for help from Pasqual'.

FLORINDO. You had better ask help from someone with more sense. *(Goes into his room.)*

TRUFFALDINO. Well if I don't show sense this time, I shall never show it again. *(Follows FLORINDO into his room.)*

SCENE IV
A Room in the House of Pantalone.

PANTALONE, the DOCTOR, Clarice, SILVIO and SMERALDINA.

PANTALONE. Come, Clarice, pull yourself together. You see that Signor Silvio has repented and asks your forgiveness. If he acted foolishly, it was all for love of you. I have forgiven him his extravagances, you ought to forgive him too.

SILVIO. Measure my agony by your own, Signora Clarice, and rest assured that I most truly love you, since 'twas the fear of losing you that rendered me distracted. Heaven desires our happiness. Do not be ungrateful for the blessings of Providence. Do not let the idea of revenge spoil the most beautiful day of your life.

LOMBARDI. I join my prayers to those of my son. Signora Clarice, my dear daughter-in-law, have pity on the poor young man; he nearly went out of his mind.

SMERALDINA. Come, dear madam, what would you? Men are all cruel to us, some more, some less. They demand the most absolute fidelity, and on the least shadow of suspicion they bully and ill-treat and are like to murder us. Well, you have got to marry one or another of them some day, so I say to you as one says to sick people—since you have got to take your nasty medicine, take it.

PANTALONE. There, do you hear that? Smeraldina calls matrimony medicine. You must not think it is poison. *(Aside to LOMBARDI.)* We must try to cheer her up.

LOMBARDI. Certainly 'tis not poison, nor even nasty medicine. Matrimony is a lollipop, a jujube, a lozenge!

SILVIO. But dear Clarice, won't you say a word? I know I deserve to be punished by you, but of your mercy, punish me with hard words rather than with silence. Behold me at your feet; have pity upon me.

CLARICE. *(To SILVIO with a sigh.)* Cruel!

PANTALONE. *(Aside to LOMBARDI.)* You heard that little sigh? A good sign.

LOMBARDI. *(Aside to SILVIO.)* Strike while the iron is hot.

SMERALDINA. *(Aside.)* A sigh is like lightning; it promises rainfall.

SILVIO. If I could think that you desired my blood to avenge my supposed cruelty, I give it you with all my heart. But, oh God! instead of the blood of my veins, accept, I beg you, that which gushes from my eyes. *(Weeps.)*

PANTALONE. Bravo! Bravo! Well said!

LOMBARDI. Capital! Capital!

CLARICE. *(Sighing as before, but more tenderly.)* Cruel!

LOMBARDI. *(Aside to PANTALONE.)* She's done to a turn.

PANTALONE. Here, come, up with you *(He raises SILVIO, takes him by the hand.)* Stand over there. *(Takes CLARICE's hand.)* And you come here too madam. Now, join your hands together again; and make peace. So no more tears, be happy, no more nonsense and Heaven bless you both.

LOMBARDI. There; 'tis done.

SMERALDINA. 'Tis done, 'tis done.

SILVIO. *(Holding Clarice's hand.)* Oh, Signora Clarice, for pity's sake—

CLARICE. Ungrateful!

SILVIO. Dearest!

CLARICE. Inhuman!

SILVIO. Beloved!

CLARICE. Monster!

SILVIO. Angel!

CLARICE. *(Sighs.)* Ah!
PANTALONE. *(Aside.)* Going, going—
SILVIO. Forgive me for the love of Heaven.
CLARICE. *(Sighs.)* I forgive you.
PANTALONE. *(Aside.)* Gone!
LOMBARDI. Come, Silvio, she has forgiven you.
SMERALDINA. The patient is ready; give her her medicine.

Enter BRIGHELLA.

BRIGHELLA. By your leave, may I come in?
PANTALONE. Pray come in, good friend Brighella. 'Twas you, was it not, that told me all these pretty stories, who assured me that that party was Signor Federigo—eh?
BRIGHELLA. My dear sir, who would not have been deceived? They were twin brother and sister, as like as two peas. In those clothes I would have wagered my head that it was he.
PANTALONE. Enough. That's all done with. What is the news?
BRIGHELLA. Signora Beatrice is here, and desires to pay her respects.
PANTALONE. Let her come in; she is most welcome.
CLARICE. Poor Signora Beatrice, I am happy to think that her troubles are over.
SILVIO. You are sorry for her?
CLARICE. I am indeed.
SILVIO. And for me?
CLARICE. Oh, cruel!
PANTALONE. *(Aside to LOMBARDI.)* You hear those loving words?
LOMBARDI. *(Aside to PANTALONE.)* Ah, my son has a way with him.
PANTALONE. My daughter, poor dear child, has a very good heart.
SMERALDINA. Yes, they will both of them do their duty by each other.

Enter BEATRICE.

BEATRICE. Ladies and gentlemen, I come to ask your pardon and forgiveness, that you should on my account have been put to inconvenience—

CLARICE. No, no, my dear; come to me. *(Embraces her.)*

SILVIO. *(Annoyed at the embrace.)* How now?

BEATRICE. *(To SILVIO.)* What! may she not even embrace a woman?

SILVIO. *(Aside.)* 'Tis those clothes again.

PANTALONE. Well, well, Signora Beatrice, I must say, for a young woman of your age you have a wonderful courage.

LOMBARDI. *(To BEATRICE.)* Too much spirit, madam.

BEATRICE. Love makes one do great things.

PANTALONE. And you have found your young gentleman at last? so I hear.

BEATRICE. Yes, Heaven has made us happy.

LOMBARDI. A nice reputation you have made yourself!

BEATRICE. Sir, you have no business with my affairs.

SILVIO. *(To LOMBARDI.)* Sir, I beg you, let everyone do as they will; do not be so put out about it. Now that I am happy, I want all the world to be happy too. Is any one else going to be married? let them all get married.

SMERALDINA. *(To SILVIO.)* What about me, sir?

SILVIO. Whom are you going to marry?

SMERALDINA. The first man that comes along, sir.

SILVIO. Find him then; I am here.

CLARICE. *(To SILVIO.)* You? what for?

SILVIO. To give her a wedding present.

CLARICE. That is no affair of yours.

SMERALDINA. *(Aside.)* She's afraid everybody will eat him. She likes the taste of him, I see.

Enter TRUFFALDINO.

TRUFFALDINO. My respects to the company.

BEATRICE. *(To TRUFFALDINO.)* Where is Signor Florindo?

TRUFFALDINO. He is here, and would like to come in, by your leave.

BEATRICE. Signor Pantalone, will you give Signor Florindo leave?

PANTALONE. Is that your young gentleman?

BEATRICE. He is going to marry me.

PANTALONE. I shall be pleased to meet him.

BEATRICE. *(To TRUFFALDINO.)* Show him in.

TRUFFALDINO. *(Aside to SMERALDINA.)* Young woman, my respects to you.

SMERALDINA. *(Aside to TRUFFALDINO.)* Pleased to see you, my little darkie.

TRUFFALDINO. We will have a talk.

SMERALDINA. What about?

TRUFFALDINO. *(Makes as though giving her a wedding-ring.)* Are you willing?

SMERALDINA. Why not?

TRUFFALDINO. We'll have a talk. *(Exits.)*

SMERALDINA. *(To CLARICE.)* Madam, with the company's leave, I want a favour of you.

CLARICE. *(Going aside to listen to SMERALDINA.)* What is it?

SMERALDINA. *(To CLARICE.)* I too am a poor young girl that would like to settle myself. There's the servant of Signora Beatrice who wants to marry me; now if you would say a kind word to his mistress, and get her to allow him to take me to wife, I should be the happiest girl in the world.

CLARICE. Dear Smeraldina, I will gladly do it. As soon as I can speak freely to Beatrice, I will certainly do so.

PANTALONE. *(To CLARICE.)* What is all this whispering about?

CLARICE. Nothing, sir. She had something to say to me.

SILVIO. *(To CLARICE.)* May I not know?

CLARICE. How inquisitive they all are! And then they talk about us women!

Enter FLORINDO shown in by TRUFFALDINO.

FLORINDO. Your most humble servant, ladies and gentleman. *(All bow and curtsey. He continues to PANTALONE.)* Are you the master of the house, sir?

PANTALONE. Yours to command, sir.

FLORINDO. Allow me, sir, to have the honour of waiting upon you this evening. I present myself by command of the Signora Beatrice, whose fortunes will be known to you, and mine too.

PANTALONE. I am happy to know you, sir, and to see you here. I congratulate you most heartily on your good fortune.

FLORINDO. Signora Beatrice is to be my wife, and if you will not disdain to do us the honour, I hope you will give away the bride.

PANTALONE. Whatever has to be done, let it be done at once. Give her your hand.

FLORINDO. Signora Beatrice, I am willing.

BEATRICE. Here is my hand, Signor Florindo.

SMERALDINA. *(Aside.)* They don't want pressing.

PANTALONE. Afterwards we will settle up our accounts. You will put yours in order. Then we will settle ours.

CLARICE. (*To BEATRICE.)* Dear friend, I congratulate you.

BEATRICE. *(To CLARICE.)* And I you with all my heart.

SILVIO. *(To FLORINDO.)* Sir, do you know me again?

FLORINDO. *(To SILVIO.)* Indeed I do, sir. You would have provoked me to a duel.

SILVIO. 'Twas to my own disaster. Here is the adversary *(Pointing to BEATRICE.)* who disarmed me and very nearly killed me.

BEATRICE. And gave you your life too, you might say.

SILVIO. 'Tis true.

CLARICE. At my entreaty.

SILVIO. That is very true.

PANTALONE. Everything is in order, everything is settled.

TRUFFALDINO. The best is yet to come, ladies and gentlemen.

PANTALONE. What is yet to come?

TRUFFALDINO. *(To FLORINDO, taking him apart.)* With your good leave, sir, one word.

FLORINDO. What do you want?

TRUFFALDINO. You remember what you promised me, sir?

FLORINDO. What did I promise? I do not recollect.

TRUFFALDINO. To ask Si'or Pantalon' for Smeraldina as my wife.

FLORINDO. Of course, now I remember. I will do so at once.

TRUFFALDINO. *(Aside.)* I too, poor man, want to put myself right with the world.

FLORINDO. Signor Pantalone, although this is the first occasion on which I have had the honour of knowing you, I make bold to desire a favour of you.

PANTALONE. You may command me, sir. I will serve you to the best of my powers.

FLORINDO. My manservant desires to marry your maid. Have you any objection to giving your consent?

SMERALDINA. *(Aside.)* Wonderful! Here's another who wants to marry me! Who the devil can he be? I wish I knew him.

PANTALONE. For my part I am agreed. *(To SMERALDINA.)* What say you, girl?

SMERALDINA. If I thought he would make a good husband—

PANTALONE. Is he a good honest man, this servant of yours?

FLORINDO. For the short time he has been with me he has certainly proved himself trusty, and he seems to be intelligent.

CLARICE. Signor Florindo, you have anticipated me in something that I ought to have done. I was to propose the marriage of my maid with the manservant of Signora Beatrice. You have asked for her for your servant, I can say no more.

FLORINDO. No, no; since you so earnestly desire this, I withdraw altogether and leave you completely free.

CLARICE. Indeed, sir, I could never permit myself to have my own wishes preferred to yours. Besides, I must admit that I am not fully authorised. Pray continue in your proposal.

FLORINDO. You say so out of courtesy, madam. Signor Pantalone, I withdraw all that I have said. I will not say another word on behalf of my servant. On the contrary, I am absolutely opposed to his marrying her.

CLARICE. If your man is not to marry her, no more shall the other man. We must be fair on both sides.

TRUFFALDINO. *(Aside.)* Here's a state of things! They pay each other compliments, and meanwhile I am left without a wife at all.

SMERALDINA. *(Aside.)* It looks as if I should have neither one nor the other.

PANTALONE. Come, we must settle it somehow. This poor girl wants to get married, let us give her either to the one or the other.

FLORINDO. Not to my man. Nothing shall induce me to do Signora Clarice an injustice.

CLARICE. Nor will I ever tolerate an injustice to Signor Florindo.

TRUFFALDINO. Sir, madam, I can settle the matter myself.

(With his usual air of great ingenuity.) Si'or Florindo, did you not ask the hand of Smeraldina for your servant?

FLORINDO. I did. Did you not hear me?

TRUFFALDINO. And you, Si'ora Clarice, did you not intend Smeraldina to marry the servant of Si'ora Beatrice?

CLARICE. Most certainly I was to do so.

TRUFFALDINO. Good. Then if that is so, give me your hand, Smeraldina.

PANTALONE. And pray what right have you to ask for her hand?

TRUFFALDINO. Because I am the servant of Si'or Florindo and of Si'ora Beatrice too.

FLORINDO. What?

BEATRICE. What do you say?

TRUFFALDINO. Pray be calm. Si'or Florindo, who asked you to ask Si'or Pantalon' for Smeraldina?

FLORINDO. You did.

TRUFFALDINO. And you, Si'ora Clarice, whom had you in mind as the intended husband of Smeraldina?

CLARICE. Yourself.

TRUFFALDINO. Ergo, Smeraldina is mine.

FLORINDO. Signora Beatrice, where is your servant?

BEATRICE. Why, here! Truffaldino, of course.

FLORINDO. Truffaldino? He is my servant!

BEATRICE. Is not yours called Pasquale?

FLORINDO. Pasquale? I thought Pasquale was yours!

BEATRICE. *(To TRUFFALDINO.)* How do you explain this?

TRUFFALDINO. *(Makes silent gestures asking for forgiveness.)*

FLORINDO. You rascal!

BEATRICE. You knave!

FLORINDO. So you waited on two masters at once?

TRUFFALDINO. Yes, sir, I did, that was the very trick. I took on the job without thinking; just to see what I could do. It did not last long, 'tis true; but at any rate I can boast that nobody would ever have found me out, if I had not given myself away for love of this girl here. I have done a hard day's work, and I dare say I had my short-comings, but I hope that in consideration of the fun of the thing, all these ladies and gentlemen will forgive me.

THE END